GRANITE

PUBLISHING

2602 Dunwoody Drive
Madison, Wisconsin 53713
USA
www.climbingcentral.com
beta.climbingcentral.com

DESIGN AND PRODUCTION
Eric Landmann

EDITING
Don Hynek

FRONT COVER PHOTO
Derrik Patola on Thursday Night Whore (5.8), Orient Bay
Photographer – Nick Buda

First Printing, May, 2006

Library of Congress Cataloging in Publication Data
Editor: Don Hynek
Includes indices and maps.
1. Rock climbing – Ontario, Canada – Guidebooks.
2. Midwest, Western Ontario – Guidebooks.
I. Editor: Don Hynek
II. Granite Publishing
III. Title (Third Edition)

ISBN 0-9619571-8-2

Thunder Bay Rock

Table of Contents

The completion of this guidebook required many hours of research, photography, and (fortunately) climbing. But this guidebook would never have made it onto your bookshelf or into your pack without generous gifts of information and time from many people. Shaun Bent was the co-author of the first edition of this book, and so helped shape it into its present form. Randy Reed provided vast amounts of information, especially on Taj Mah Wall, Da Projects, Schoolhouse, Mt. Olympus, Mahkwa, First Buttress, Climbers Cliffs, The Wrinkles and Highway 61. He also helped in providing much general information about Thunder Bay climbing.

Nick Buda contributed freely from a large store of excellent pictures. Shaun Parent contributed extensive historical information related to The Bluffs, Mt. Helen, Chipmunk Rock, Dorion Towers, Caribou and Kama Bay. Dan Green contributed information on Claghorn. Chris Chapman provided material on Climbers Cliffs, and Lost Falls, and Brandon Pullan added information to Lost Falls and Silver Harbour, among other areas.

Jeff Hammerich has done significant work regarding Lost Falls, Chiller Pillar and Orient Bay. Eric Landmann, Scott Morgan, Todd Free, Steve Charlton, Jody Bernst, Scott Kress, Chris Joseph, Jarron Childs, Bryce Brown, Dave Benton, Ryan Treneer, Dylan Cummings, Don Salonen, and Rob Dynes all proved to be useful and reliable sources.

Vincent Beasse at Mountain Equipment Co-op, and Frank Pianka with the Thunder Bay Alpine Club were instrumental in helping to publish earlier versions of this guide.

Finally, thanks are due to all to all those who sent slides, prints, photos, and tidbits of information that allowed myself and a number of remote editors (New Zealand, Western Canada, Pickle Lake, NWT and Wisconsin) to combine all the information into a useful and worthwhile book. It serves to document the tremendous amount of development that has occurred over the past decade and provides a benchmark for an entire new body of climbers.

Introduction

Where are the Cliffs?

The Thunder Bay area is centrally located (depending on your point of view) along the Trans-Canada highway, seven hours (670 km) east of Winnipeg and seven hours (650 km) west of Sault Ste. Marie. For Americans, the city is 6.5 hours north of Minneapolis/St. Paul, on I-35 & Highway 61. The bulk of the climbing areas in this guide are within 30 minutes to an hour from Thunder Bay with a few exceptions. See the locator map for each area in their respective sections of the guide. An overview map is on the back of the guide.

All the location descriptions in this guide are in reference to the corner of the Harbour Expressway and Highway 11/17 in Thunder Bay. I chose this location as a landmark to base the route descriptions from. as it is located centrally in Thunder Bay and is easily found. Thunder Bay is located in Northwestern Ontario, on the north shore of Lake Superior on Highway 11/17, 1,467 km northwest of Toronto, and 709 km east of Winnipeg.

From the Toronto area, plan on a 16- to 19-hour drive. Follow Highway 400 northbound through Barrie and North Bay. Then take Highway 11 (1,672 km), or Highway 17 through Sault Ste. Marie (1,467 km). The route through Sault Ste. Marie follows the shore of Lake Superior, offering a more scenic drive. From the Winnipeg area, plan a 7- to 8-hour drive (709km). Follow the Trans Canada Highway east. From the Minneapolis area you're looking at about a 6- to 7-hour drive (581km/361mi). Follow Highway 69 North to the border then continue on Highway 61 to Thunder Bay.

All of the established areas have easy two-wheel drive access from the Trans-Canada Highway. Approaches range from being able to belay off your bumper to a two-hour hike. Approaches are often through beautiful boreal forests and many walls are situated on high slopes. Some of the climbing areas are located on private property, or property owned by the Nishnawbiaski First Nations. Other areas are on municipal property, or more often, on Crown land.

This introduction is intended to help both the seasoned regular and the first time visitor understand how to use the book and how to minimize environmental impacts. There is also information on how to get to the areas, ratings, local ethics, weather, camping, and where to stay and eat.

This book builds on several previous works. The genesis of this book came from work done by Shaun Bent and and the present author in 1996. Randy Reed assisted greatly in expanding that work for a 2003 edition. We all were assisted greatly by a number of earlier works and assembled notes, from fellow climbers noted in the history below.

Alpine Club members practice with the Orient Bay Emergency Evacuation Kit (OBEEK).

The 25 climbing areas in Thunder Bay now include almost 600 routes, in sport and traditional style, single and multi-pitch routes. Most of the areas listed have barely been scratched in terms of their potential routes. If Orient Bay or Squaw Bay were the only crags in the area, climbers would still be busy doing new routes in the Northwest for years to come.

New route information, corrections, and updates can either be directed to the Thunder Bay Section of the Alpine Club of Canada http://www.acctbay.ca/ or to the author by email at alxj@yahoo.com. If all else fails, messages about Thunder Bay rock can be broadcast via the blog posted at http://tbayrock.yourhomeplanet.com. Please also report new routes on the new route form at Climbing Central's beta site http://beta.climbingcentral.com/. The beta site contains route information and photo galleries.

WARNING

If you are reading this book, you probably know this, but we have to say it; Climbing is an inherently dangerous sport where injuries can be serious or fatal. The author of this guide and the various contributors do not guarantee the accuracy of any information provided herein, nor does he take any responsibility for any actions taken based on this guide's contents. No guidebook can be 100% correct, and a book certainly can't adjust for local conditions or weather. Make prudent decisions based on conditions observed first hand. Hiking, camping, and such are undertaken entirely at one's own risk (Canada has a LOT fewer lawyers than the U.S.) and in any place that does not present a fire hazard.

The Thunder Bay area operates on the 911 system for all emergencies. Do **not** depend on cellular phone service. It is limited throughout the area and may well not work at a number of these climbing areas.

If you find yourself in need of a rescue, contact the police who will deploy an emergency response team to your site. Use the directions within this book to assist the emergency response team in finding your location.

Many of the routes within this guide have only seen a single or handful of ascents. In several cases the first ascent team did not remove any loose rock or lichen, thus leaving subsequent parties to face treacherous conditions, or the daunting task of cleaning the route properly. With this in mind, the use of a helmet is strongly recommended.

Self-driving Red Head construction anchors (5/16" x 1.5") are in place on many of the routes established in the early 1980s, as was the norm at the time. These anchors in many cases do not have any hangers or bolts in the sleeves, and time and weather have taken their toll. So, be suspicious at the least. Check old bolts for cracks, excessive corrosion, and brittleness. Avoid banging on old bolts, as this will further weaken them. The pitons used during this time frame have also suffered the same torture from the elements. If there is any doubt, back them up or replace them.

Another consideration to bear in mind is that there is no formal high angle rescue team in the Thunder Bay area. So if you are venturing to some of the more remote locations in this book be prepared to perform your own rescue if the need arises.

OBEEK (Orient Bay Emergency Evacuation Kit)

With the above in mind, the Thunder Bay section of the Alpine Club of Canada has located emergency evacuation equipment in the Orient Bay corridor to expedite the extraction of any injured person. In the event of an emergency, the victim can be extracted to the highway while waiting for an EMS response. The following equipment is now available for emergency use by anyone needing it:

1 International Stretcher System, yellow jacket litter + 4 hoisting straps
1 Ministry of Health spec backboard + 4 quick release straps
1 stiffneck collar, adjustable
1 pocket mask w/O2 filter, valve
Misc. emergency blankets, padding, and tape.

This equipment is located at the Trans Canada Power Plant, adjacent to Compressor Station #75. This is across from the Gomar Falls ice climbing area, or about 5 km south of Reflection Wall. The gate phone is answered 24/7, and staff at the plant will provide the kit and initiate a 911 response. Contact the Plant Manager at 807-885-5571. For more information from the Alpine Club, contact Frank Pianka, Thunder Bay Section representative, at (807) 577-7950.

A Short History of Thunder Bay Rock Climbing

Thunder Bay is living up to its name of "The Mecca of Ontario Climbing." Rock and ice climbers have been ascending this region's Canadian Shield for 30 years.

Although a few rumours and some obviously old pitons may well date back before the late '70s, it seems that Paul Dedi, then a resident of Thunder Bay, was the first local to attend one of Richard Latus's climbing workshops in 1979 through the city Parks and Recreation Department. He, teacher Doug Nichols and some Lakehead students including Shaun Parent, Randy Frietag, Paul Mahoney and Bill Ostrom began cleaning The Bluffs in the fall of 1979. As their enthusiasm grew, exploration expanded to Climbers Cliffs, Pearl, The Sleeping Giant, and Silver Harbour. In the fall of 1979, while climbing in the area around what is now "Go Joe" at Pass Lake, two climbers were nearly struck by a huge (one ton?) block of rock that fell off the overhang. This was only one of several near-misses, and the area's small climbing

An early trip to Dorion Towers (circa 1990). Left to right: Bill Konkol, Smitty, Frank Pianka, Shaun Parent.

community came to believe that the area was dangerous for climbing.

Paul Dedi, Shaun Parent, Bill Ostrom, and Randy Frietag formed the Face High climbing club in 1980, which attracted several members. They had a vast area of virgin rock to explore. Classics such as "Go Joe" and the five pitches of "Discovery" were climbed.

The original pioneers of rock climbing in Thunder Bay were all students in the Lakehead University Outdoor Recreation program (excluding Paul Dedi, who was a Thunder Bay resident). These pioneers mainly climbed The Bluffs, using them as a teaching site for courses and clinics.

The first ever compilation of rock routes in the Thunder Bay area was Shaun Parent's 1983 *Climbing Guide to the Thunder Bay Area*. That guide listed 92 routes, 55 at The Bluffs, and the rest at Claghorn, Climbers Cliffs, the Sleeping Giant, and a few other areas. This, the first of numerous Parent guides, also notes that there were four lead climbers in the entire area. A 1984 second edition, published with funding from the Alpine Club of Canada added new routes, but no new areas.

While new routes continued to be claimed in the other known areas throughout the early 1980s, this small group of climbers began to explore other sites. In 1981, Tom Morrissey from Atikokan introduced the Thunder Bay climbers to the newly abandoned Caylan open pit. It was here that the climbers found a 100-metre-high wall of slabby volcanic rocks. The "pit" was climbed until the mid-'80s and produced many excellent face climbs including "The Pit and the Pendulum" (5.10). As the mine filled,

Randy Reed and Steve Charlton at the Taj Mah Wall after a day of route development, Sept. 1999.

the Caylan wall was finally submerged in 1985, leading to the loss of what had become one of the finest rock climbing areas in the north. Mt. Helen began receiving attention in 1984. The Dorion Tower was discovered as Dave Pugliese and Shaun Parent returned from a reconnaissance flight to Orient Bay seeking ice routes. Dave first spotted the large free-standing pillar, and they made a low fly-by, and took a photo of the site. A week later Shaun, Dave and Peter Powell returned for the first ascent after spending several hours bushwhacking to find its exact location.

In 1982, the Thunder Bay Alpine Group was formed as a probationary section of the Alpine Club of Canada. In 1983, the club, under the chairmanship of Neil Gilson, made application to be recognized as a full section of the national club (Thunder Bay section). Shaun Parent and Joanne Murphy headed to the annual meeting in Canmore in the spring of 1983 with the application and a short presentation on why a section should be represented in Thunder Bay. In the spring of 1983, the national club recognized the Thunder Bay club. With the departure of Neil Gilson and most of the executive officers in 1983, the club was in a state of limbo for some time. It remained in existence only thanks to the efforts of Peter Powell, until it was revived when Dave Robinson, a Professor in Outdoor Recreation at Lakehead University, took over as Section Chairman for a season. The club was again active but not enthusiastic until the early 1990s.

The next guidebook to surface was published in 1989 by Chris Wrazej and Marc Barbeau entitled *Pass Lake... The Next Generation*. This book highlights the efforts projected by the authors, and their very active climbing partners. The following year another guidebook, *A Guide to Rock Climbing at the Scenic Bluffs of Thunder Bay* was released by Shaun Parent. This guide listed over 100 routes at the Centennial Park Bluffs.

At least two waves of University – students breathed life into the club in the early and late 1990s, resulting in two significant expansions of climbing in the area, with a guide to Silver Harbour and the newly-developed rock routes in the Orient Bay Corridor. Some of the other club activities over this period included the OBEEK project and bringing the Banff Film Fest to Thunder Bay in 1992. The festival celebrated its 10th anniversary in Thunder Bay with special guests Chic Scott and Barry Blanchard present to witness what is now considered the model for film fest presentations. During this period Frank Pianka's dedication to weekly club outings to the Bluffs was central in introducing young people to rock climbing in the area.

Julian Anfossi was an LU Outdoor Rec. student in the early 1990s and wrote a climbing guide to Silver Harbour as his graduation project. In 1992, two climbers from Holland visited the Bluffs and climbed "The Flying Dutchman" (5.12a). The bolting of this route caused a serious verbal battle regarding the ethics of bolting the route at the Bluffs. That debate influenced the general style of current route development, bringing a largely traditional ground-up style.

The Squaw Bay area was first explored by Dave Pagel (currently of Duluth, Minnesota), Peter Powell and Shaun Parent. Rob Dynes, Don Salonen, Chris Joseph and Shaun Bent developed a number of intermediate routes in McKenzie in 1994–95. The area is now closed; it is private property.

Outward Bound classes have used the Claghorn/Black Sturgeon crags since the 1980s. They fixed a number of single-pitch climbs with permanent gear. Ryan Treneer, Dan Green, Scott Fettles and a few others have put up a few new routes in this area recently. One of the long-eyed routes to fall recently is Silver Harbour Dream Line. Originally an aid climb, this route was free climbed and graded 5.11b. And Chris Chapman, with the Climbers Cliffs now in his backyard, has put up some new routes with Jeff Hammerich and Randy Reed to complement the early 1980s development. The Jolly Jester Wall presents an as-yet unfreed challenge, (tentatively named "Electric Gigolo") which will likely become the first 5.13 in the region.

Since 1997, focus has turned to the Orient Bay Corridor. Randy Reed, Steve Charlton, Jody Bernst and Matt Pellett have led the development on the 80+ metre cliffs with a ground-up approach to many ascents. They take pride in their "tread lightly" attitude and the work they have put in, sometimes in the middle of winter, to blaze and reinforce trails. "The Colossus" is perhaps the best representation of the tremendous climbing there with an incredible undercling traverse to finish off the 40 metre second pitch. As well, Jody Bernst sent "Temple of Zeus" (5.10+) as an onsight first ascent, which is perhaps the most incredible climbing event in the area to date. Still, the Orient Bay Corridor has enormous amounts of unclimbed rock. Randy Reed, Steve Charlton, and Todd Free have ascended a 3-pitch route they've called "Passage to Valhalla," which will likely become one of the finest free climbs in Ontario with sustained 5.12 trad climbing on the 1st pitch.

Other individuals contributed to route development during the 1990s, including Shaun Bent (Mt. Godfrey), Eric Furlotte, Scott Morgan, Corey Davis, Dave Nix, Scott Hamilton, Mike O'Brien and Mike Holowaty. These people, along with many others, have put up many high-end routes throughout the region.

And even more recently, the Lost Falls area was explored for rock climbing potential after some observant ice climbers identified numerous potential lines. Unbelievably, some of the most obvious routes were left untouched until 2002.

Border Considerations

It's easy to not pay a lot of attention to crossing the longest unfortified border in the world, but U.S. citizens need to keep a few issues in mind. Transit back and forth from the U.S. is no longer the simple formality it was just a few years ago. Getting into Canada is not really rigorous, but getting back to the U.S. is far more controlled. The Pigeon River crossing on Highway 61 between Minnesota and Ontario is open 24 hours. Canadian Customs will require a valid photo ID. Coming back to the U.S., expect to be asked for a photo ID and proof of U.S. citizenship such as a birth certificate, naturalization certificate, or expired U.S. passport. By December 31, 2007, all U.S. citizens will be required to present a valid passport or other authorized document establishing identity and U.S. citizenship in order to depart and enter the United States. And remember, cigars made in Cuba are available in Canada but are not allowed into the U.S!

No visa is needed for U.S. citizens to stay in Canada for less than 180 days. Canada law provides that anyone with a criminal record (including a DWI charge) may be excluded or removed from Canada.

Gear and equipment brought into Canada for use is not subject to duty or taxes. Some foods are subject to restrictions, or are not permitted, including perishable items, vegetables, meat and dairy products. For more information on Customs' regulations, sales taxes and visitor tax rebate in Canada, you can visit http://www.ccra-adrc.gc.ca/. Visitors of age (19 in most of Ontario!) may bring either 1.5 litres of wine, 1.14 litres of liquor, or one case, or the equivalent, of beer or ale. Drink wisely; driving while intoxicated (DWI) in Canada is a serious offense.

Tobacco products for personal use are restricted to up to 200 cigarettes, 50 cigars, or 200 grams (7 ounces) of loose tobacco. Additional quantities are subject to duties, provincial fees and taxes. Firearms are strictly controlled in Canada. All hunting firearms and small amounts of ammunition must be declared in writing using a Non-Resident Firearm Declaration form. Handguns, fireworks, and other pyrotechnics are prohibited, except for highway flares.

American residents who spend more than 48 hours in Canada are allowed to take goods purchased in Canada worth up to US$400 back into the U.S. You may take advantage of this exemption only once every 30 days. Members of a single family, travelling together and living in the same residence, are allowed to pool their exemptions to cover their combined purchases. U.S. citizens are allowed one litre of alcohol, 100 cigars or one carton of 200 cigarettes within one exemption.

Your pets are welcome, too, but animals from the U.S. are required to have a signed and dated (in the previous 36 months) veterinarian vaccination certificate for rabies. Seeing-eye dogs face no restrictions.

Most U.S. health insurance plans do not automatically provide coverage in Canada. You should consult with your medical insurance company prior to traveling abroad to confirm whether their policy applies overseas and whether it will cover emergency expenses such as a medical evacuation. Your car insurance may extend north of the border, but Canada requires all drivers to have proof of insurance, a Canadian Non-resident Insurance Card, with them. Your insurance company can provide one, but it may take five days to process, so plan ahead. Getting into an accident without it will make life very complicated.

U.S. driver's licenses are valid in Canada. Unless otherwise posted, the maximum speed limit in Canada is 50km/hr in cities and 80km/hr on highways. On rural highways, the posted speed limit may be 100km/hr (approximately 60 miles/hr). Seat belt use is mandatory for all passengers. Drivers are required to keep their headlights on during the day. It is illegal to take automobile radar detectors into Ontario, regardless of whether they are used or not. Police may confiscate radar detectors, operational or not, and may impose substantial fines.

Camping and General Services

Much of the area described in this book is on publicly-owned and generally unrestricted land. Hiking, camping, and such are undertaken at one's own risk (Canada has a **lot** fewer lawyers than the U.S.) and are generally allowed in any place that does not present a fire or traffic hazard. However, Canadians have nothing but scorn for what they call the "half-tank tourist" – the guy who tops off his gas tank and buys a full load of beer and bait in Grand Portage, and then drives only half a tankful into Canada so he can bush camp free for a week. So the MNR recently instituted the Crown Land Camping Permit.

Non-citizens camping on Crown land are expected to purchase a camping permit, at $10C per person per night. The fee does not apply in any established and operating private or park campground, or when being supported by a local guide service. Note that you are expected to get a Crown land permit when camping in a park that is otherwise closed. It's not clear that the permit is enforced heavily, if at all.

In general, prices in Canada are higher than in the U.S., especially on gas and alcohol. While it's good to support the local economy, a little planning goes a long way. The Canadian dollar is stronger than it's been in decades, and to add insult to injury, border-area merchants will be happy to exchange your U.S. dollars on the spot – for a 10 percent fee. Your bank can probably exchange currency inexpensively, and many credit card companies offer reasonable exchange rates as well. Do some homework.

Canadians pay a sizable Goods and Services Tax (GST), on the order of 7 or 8 percent. U.S. citizens have to pay it, too. However, you can get a refund of all GST paid, if you apply from the U.S. within 60 days of leaving Canada. Duty Free shops at the border can refund GST taxes on the spot, if you fill out the application form in the pamphlet on GST Taxes that they all carry. You must have spent more than $100, have original receipts, and be claiming less than $500 in refunds. A larger claim can be made only by mail, from your residence.

Climate, Flora and Fauna

The climbing season runs generally from April to October. Reading this material closely may reveal that an unusual number of first ascents happen in April and November. The odd sun-facing cliff (especially Pass Lake) may well be climbed during warm days in December and even January.

In early season, approaches and base areas can be wet and muddy. Locals have perfected an approach technique that works well; they hike in wearing pac boots, with a pair of rock shoes that can be worn all day substituted for the much-too-warm felt liners. You will spot the true locals when you see a climber step out of their pac boots up onto a route, and then lower back into them coming down off the route!

Other than bears, bugs are the only real enemy. Blackflies and mosquitoes often arrive in late May, peak in June and July, and can last into August. However, exposed rock faces on windy days in areas like Squaw Bay, Pass Lake and Sleeping Giant offer opportunities to escape their wrath. Lost Falls, Climbers Cliffs, The Bluffs, Silver

FRANK PIANKA COLLECTION

Peregrine falcon banding at Old Woman Bay, June 2005. Left to right: Rod Swatton, Brian Ratcliff, Frank Pianka.

Harbour and Claghorn can be particularly buggy in June and July. Remember that nylon does not respond well when exposed to DEET mosquito repellants.

All of the area in this book is black bear country. Bears rarely bother climbers, hikers or other day travelers. However, all food is of course fair game, as far as a bear is concerned. The campsites commonly used by area climbers all have trees suitable for hanging bear bags.

The Thunder Bay area has seen a steady increase in peregrine falcons over the last ten years. Areas that hold nesting falcons are not officially closed to climbing, as is common in other areas. However, climbers should be suitably cautious if they are climbing in an area where nesting birds may be disturbed (from about mid-June to the end of July). The most sensitive area for raptors is probably at Squaw Bay near the climb "Cedar Haven," where falcons have nested repeatedly year after year. You may also see or hear them in the Lost Falls area, the Sleeping Giant or near Dorion Tower.

If you accidentally disturb nesting falcons, they will clearly display their agitation. You should move out of the area and avoid it for the duration of the nesting season, and advise other climbers to do the same. The Thunder Bay section of the Alpine Club of Canada is involved with peregrine falcon banding, through Project Peregrine. They maintain information about sensitive areas on the club website http://www.acctbay.ca/. A call to the club at (807) 577-7950 will also link you to people with up-to-date information.

Routes, Ratings and Climbing Style

While route ratings are always only a general guide to a climb's difficulty, many of the ratings in this book are even less precise than typical. Some of the routes in this book have seen only a few ascents, so ratings may well be based on only a few people's opinions. Subsequent route cleaning may have made routes much harder (or easier) than previous (in some cases only) ascents.

Note also that a sizable number of routes in the area are "mixed" sport/trad routes, with a few bolts placed on a route that generally needs gear. The bolts are often placed to protect crux moves, or areas where clean pro is hard to come by.

5.1 – 5.5 Beginners
5.7 – 5.7 Easy, relatively straightforward climbing
5.8 – 5.9 Challenging, especially when multi-pitch climbs and leading
5.10 Difficult, often requires substantial experience
5.11 Hard, often requires training and experience
5.12 Expert
5.13 There is one potential 5.13 in the region; Electric Gigolo, 5.13a

+ indicates the route has one particular committing or tricky move

R indicates a runout or hard-to-protect lead where the leader may be injured if they fall

X indicates extreme danger, possibly of death, if the leader were to fall

A1 Easy aid: placements are straightforward and solid. No risk of big air. Example: Right Hand Man Direct

A2 Moderate aid: two to three tenuous placements above good pro, with no bad landings. Example: American Demon

A3 Hard aid: involves some ingenuity or several tenuous placements in a row, with otherwise decent placements. A mistake in the wrong place could be a problem. Example: Test of Patience

C0 Clean aid: Absolutely bomber nut, or pulling on a bolt.

C1 Excellent clean aid placements, beginner territory

C2 Good clean aid: Generally solid placements, but may be time consuming or require some creative nut work.

 Trad route

 Sport route

 Mixed route (some fixed and some trad gear needed)

Quality Ratings

This guide uses a 3-star system to indicate routes worth doing. Of course, this rating is even more subjective than the difficulty rating. Unrated routes may be of low quality, but are many times just unknown; too few climbers have been there to make a rating. These are subjective (many of these ratings are from first ascents) and may ignore some real gems! Poor, dirty or dangerous routes are generally indicated as such in the route description.

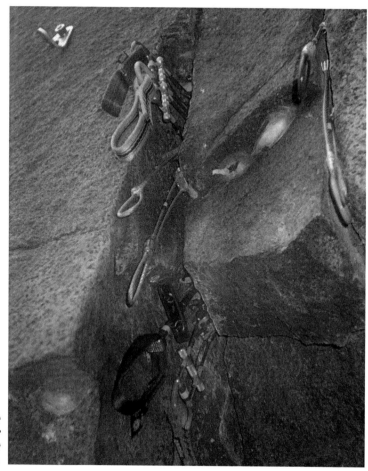

*Is this bolt
necessary?
One placement at
Silver Harbour.*

no rating   (lack of information, or a poor-quality route)

★   worth doing

★ ★   a good to great route

★ ★ ★   one of the best routes for its grade in the area.

First Ascents

Generally, the history of Thunder Bay climbing is pretty well known. Ascent history
that could be found is included where it was available. Generally, the first ascent (FA)
is by the first climber to have climbed the route in question clean, that is, with no falls.
Whatever style a first ascentionist used (i.e. top-roping, lead climb, aid cllimb, etc) is
reported. Red-point leads, "free" first ascents, (FFA) are noted in this book, as they are
deserving of such recognition as per other guides and to preserve the history of each
route.

Topo Symbols

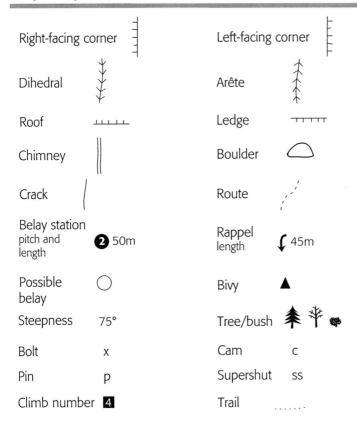

Right-facing corner

Dihedral

Roof

Chimney

Crack

Belay station
pitch and   ❷ 50m
length

Possible
belay

Steepness   75°

Bolt   X

Pin   p

Climb number **4**

Left-facing corner

Arête

Ledge

Boulder

Route

Rappel
length   ⌡ 45m

Bivy   ▲

Tree/bush

Cam   c

Supershut   ss

Trail   . . . .

Abbreviations

chim	chimney
p	fixed piton
ow	offwidth
lb	lieback
R	runout (dangerous)

Conversions

100 feet	30.5 meters
50 yards	45.7 meters
1 foot	0.305 meters
1 inch	2.54 centimetres
1 mile	1.61 kilometres
50 metres	164.0 feet
60 metres	196.9 feet
1 kilometre	0.621 miles

Fahrenheit (°F) to Celsius (°C):
$$°C = (°F - 32) / 1.8$$
Celsius (°C) to Fahrenheit (°F):
$$°F = (°C \times 1.8) + 32$$

New Routes/Development

Climbing areas have already been closed in Thunder Bay due to the visual impacts of bolts, so carefully consider if your project deserves to be bolted, and try not to let the excitement of a new route bias your judgment. Bolting face climbs at the Centennial Park Bluffs is strongly discouraged, since the area is heavily used, and the routes are relatively short and easily toproped.

Establishing new routes in the Thunder Bay area presents some interesting and often dangerous challenges. The rock here is for the most part covered in lichen, which takes a tremendous amount of scrubbing and scraping to remove. To wear out half a dozen wire brushes scrubbing a route is not unheard of. Some have even taken up to 10 days to clean.

New routes in this area of severe climate and few climbers are generally abundant with loose rock. A massive block may be precariously perched and come off with a gentle push, astonishing the climber on how it possibly could have stayed there in the first place. First ascents often involve a crowbar, or several, to remove the blocks. In extreme cases a car scissor jack has been used.

Needless to say, the climber who chooses to establish a new route here puts him or herself in a potentially dangerous environment and should exercise sound judgment when cleaning a route. Because of the hazards involved with pioneering a new route here, the top-down method of cleaning a route has become the usual method of choice. It is sometimes impractical, given the difficulty of access to the top of some areas. Although a ground-up first ascent is certainly more respectable, top-down cleaning enables the climber to do a more thorough job of cleaning a route instead of just climbing through a bunch of loose, dirty rock, naming and grading it, and moving on to the next death trap. (This was the case with many of the early routes in this area.) No one here will criticize you for cleaning a route on rappel, but establishing a new route without thoroughly cleaning it provides little enjoyment for successive parties and will certainly not enhance the quality of climbing in the Thunder Bay area.

New route information, corrections, and updates can either be directed to the Thunder Bay Section of the Alpine Club of Canada http://www.acctbay.ca/ or to the author by email at alxj@yahoo.com. If all else fails, messages about Thunder Bay rock can be broadcast via the blog posted at http://tbayrock.yourhomeplanet.com.Be sure to include such information as the name of the route, the ratings, type of protection, date of the first ascent, and the full names of the first ascent party. Also, it is important to include any topos, photos of the route, maps, as well as a thorough description of the route. Please also report new routes on the new route form at Climbing Central's beta site http://beta.climbingcentral.com/. The beta site contains route information and photo galleries.

The use of GPS to locate climbing areas has become increasingly popular. GPS can now be used to locate any point on earth to within about +/- 15m. We can expect to see GPS coordinates for climbing areas and even specific routes collected and made available over the Internet to simplify the challenge of getting to the climb. If you can provide GPS information for your area or route, give the full UTM coordinates, including the map datum used.

Aside from new route information, any corrections to this book or missing information on first ascents of existing routes would be greatly appreciated.

The first ascents of routes are respectively the right of the individual(s) who put effort into cleaning it. By jumping in, and not respecting the efforts of the person working on the new route, you are robbing the person of the fruit of their effort and eliminating motivation to establish new climbs. Climbers attempting a project usually tag the route in some manner, often projects will have gear in situ. Please don't remove it, as the locals deal harshly with thieves. If you come across a route marked as a project please respect the efforts of the person(s) working on the climb and come back when it's been completed. If a project is not marked, then it is assumed to be an "open project" and anyone is welcome to the first free ascent.

As for bolting, climbers in Thunder Bay generally use the following guidelines:

— use bolts only where natural protection is non-existent
— use only stainless steel bolts 3/8" x 2-3/4" or larger, placed in excellent quality rock
— carefully consider the clipping stance and rope line
— try to use hangers the same colour as the rock
— at stations, use only rappel hangers, leave no webbing
— fill all old bolt holes
— do not add bolts to existing routes, unless it is for the purpose of upgrading (replacing old or suspect bolts)
— do not bolt existing toprope problems
— ground-up bolting off of hooks is bold and admirable; however, attention to clipping stances is important to leave a reasonable route
— if possible, toprope sport climbing projects to ensure proper bolt placements
— it is generally acceptable to place new route bolts or belay stations within reach of an existing climb

Retro-bolting or placing bolts after a route has already seen a first ascent (i.e, "Galaxian" at The Bluffs) without consent from the route's first ascendant is considered unethical. The climber that would do something like that might even chip holds on a route! Drop a toprope on it, or do another one of the tons of climbs in this guide. Destroying that history and legacy for future climbers with a dotted line of bolts is disgraceful. If a route was lead ground up, with the leader bolting on lead, the bolt placements may not be ideal (i.e., "Temple of Zeus" and a number of climbs at Orient Bay). Give the leader due credit, and leave the route as it was led. In order to preserve the first ascent conditions, only replacement of fixed placements and upgrading belay stations is acceptable.

"It's not what you climb that counts, it's how you climb it." – Peter Croft

Accommodations

The Lakehead area is abundant with cheap places to stay, or if the wallet is fat, you can also find accommodation to suit your particular taste. Several motels, bed and breakfasts, and campgrounds are located directly off of Highway 11/17. Other motels and hotels can be found by taking a short drive down any of the main streets in town. Certainly, there is always the option of camping out under the stars. The only area that is well suited for this is the Taj Mah Wall, at Orient Bay. At the Taj there is a welcoming little camping area for those who prefer to bivy out. As for the rest of the areas, some are on private or First Nations property, so check it out with the landowners – prior. In any case be discreet, and follow the old adage: "leave only footprints and take only memories."

The following accommodations are relatively close to the climbing areas found within this book.

McCollum's Reflection Lake Cabins (807) 885-3361 – 2km from the Taj Mah Wall at Orient Bay. Small cabin rentals at reasonable rates. Ask Sharon if you can fire up the sauna!

Longhouse Village Hostel (807) 983-2042 – located about 1 km from Silver Harbour on Lakeshore Drive.

KOA (RV camping) (807) 683-6221 – Just east of Thunder Bay at the corner of Hwy 11/17 and Spruce River Road.

Normandie Hotel (807) 887-2448 – Downtown Nipigon, 20 minutes from Orient Bay. Has a bar and Bavarian restaurant.

Pass Lake Campground (807) 977-2646 – Across the road from the Pass Lake climbing area, this is the perfect spot to camp if you plan to climb there for several days.

Marie Louise Campground (807) 977-2526 – Located within the splendor of Sleeping Giant Provincial Park; backcountry permits are also available.

Restaurants

Here a few suggestions on where to get some grub while you're visiting Thunder Bay.

Seattle's Best Coffeehouse, 820 Red River Road or 588 Arthur St. W – Great coffee and desserts in a pleasant atmosphere.

Hoito, 314 Bay St. – This is a Thunder Bay classic for breakfast, offering authentic Scandinavian cuisine.

Broadway Variety, 1828 Broadway Ave. – A little East Indian restaurant in the back of a convenience store. Don't be fooled by appearance, this is an excellent spot. With outstanding food and good prices, one of the author's favorites.

Cronos Bookstore Café, 433 Syndicate Ave. S – A mellow little Greek café/bookstore with kind of a jazz character. It's a perfect place for latte or lunch, with superb gyros, falafel and milkshakes.

Calabria, 66 Court St. S – A nice Italian restaurant, with lunch buffet Wednesday through Friday, 12 till 2.

Nipigon Café, downtown Nipigon – Specializing in Greek food, and the author's first choice for eats in Nipigon.

If the budget allows treat yourself to some fine dining at:

Bistro One, 276 Cumberland N, or Giorg Restaurante, 114 Syndicate Ave. N

Other Services

Kangas Sauna, 379 Oliver Rd. – A great place to relax after a hard day of climbing.

Information Services, Terry Fox Lookout – from the corner of the Harbour Expressway and Highway 11/17 in Thunder Bay, follow Highway 11/17 east for 13.6 km. This little turnout is also the home of some decent bouldering.

The Pagoda – Canada's oldest operational tourist information center, is located at the corner of Red River Road and Water Street in the downtown section of the north end of the city.

Other Sources of Information and History

Climbing Guide to the Thunder Bay Area (1st edition, 1983; 2nd edition, 1984) Shaun Parent

Pass Lake - The Next Generation: A Guidebook to One of Northern Ontario's Leading Rock Climbing Spots (2nd ed.), Chris Wrajez & Mark Barbeau, 1989.

Manitoba and Northwestern Ontario Rock Climbing Guide, Alpine Club of Canada, Manitoba Section, 1989.

A Guide to Rock Climbing Routes at the Scenic Bluffs of Thunder Bay, S. Parent, 1990.

Climbing Route Cards: Mt. Helen, The Canine, Pearl Road Cut. S. Parent, 1990.

Silver Harbour Rock: A Climber's Guide, Julian Anfossi, 1993.

Crimp 'zine, Scott Hamilton, early 1990s?.

Bouldering at the Bluffs, Toivo Koivukoski, 1995?

Ontario's Finest Rock Climbs, Dave Smart, 1998.

Thunder Bay Scrambles on the Nor'westers, Leo Tardiff.

Notes & Field Data of Climbing in the Thunder Bay Area (a compilation), S. Parent, 2003.

Alpine Club of Canada - Thunder Bay Section, http://www.acctbay.ca/

Climbing Central, information on rock and ice climbing in the Midwest, http://www.climbingcentral.com. Includes Forums for posting new routes and getting local beta. The Beta site has a new route reporting form, route information, ratings, and photo galleries rock and ice climbs throughout Western Ontario and the Midwest U.S. It is found at http://beta.climbingcentral.com/.

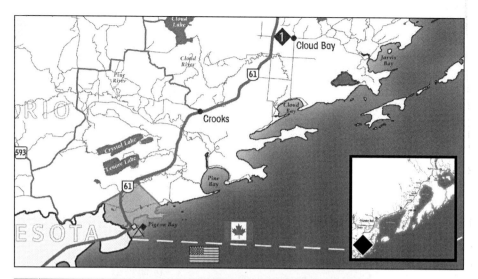

Route Character: Sport – 0, Trad – 2, Mixed – 0, Toprope – 0, Multi-pitch – 0

Difficulty: 5.9 – 1, 5.10 – 1.

Getting There: This area is about 45 minutes south of Thunder Bay on Highway 61, past the road to the Boy Scout camp. It is the only long stretch of cliff visible from the road in the area.

This sizable cliff has a variety of steep dihedrals and corner cracks. There is some good rock on 25-metre cliffs that stretch for a kilometre. Only a few routes have been done in this area, since these cliffs are believed to be located on private property. Scott Morgan and Randy Reed did a few routes here in 1997, and Shaun Parent, Bill Ostrum and Paul Dedi were likely exploring this area at even an earlier date.

It might well be worth the effort to pursue permission to climb this private property. There are two series of walls, one a thin plate about half a metre thick at the top, detached from the main wall directly behind it. All three cliff surfaces have potential routes. These routes are located on the left end of the cliff.

1 **Farewell Friends**   25 Metres   5.10

This route follows a nice big-hands (four to five inch) crack. FA: Scott Morgan, Randy Reed, May 1997.

2 **Black Fly**   25 Metres   5.9

Starts on shale, but becomes more solid in the center. Leading this route requires extra hand and fist-sized pieces. FA: S. Morgan, R. Reed (toprope), May 1997.

Note: At Cloud Bay Road, a great cliff is located right beside the road. There is no history to date of it having been explored.

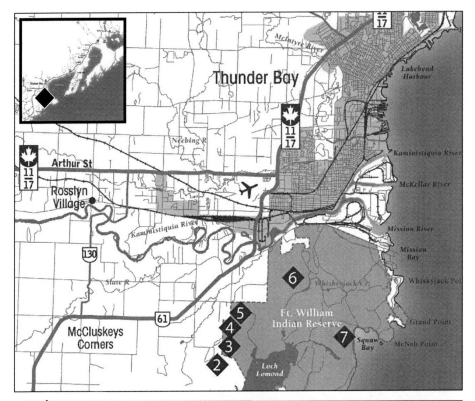

◆2 Loch Lomond

In the late 1970s, Richard Latus and a few of his climbing class students explored a number of local crags, including Loch Lomond. They did about 10 routes on these hard-to-access cliffs, but there is no detailed record of them. Climbers that venture to the area will find some pins and lost stoppers left behind by Paul Dedi, Shaun Parent and a few other climbers, from their exploratorty climbs in 1979, 1980, and 1981. The rock is generally described as loose, however some good cracks apparently exist. To find Loch Lomond, drive south out of Thunder Bay on Mountain Rd. and then turn right onto Mt. McKay Lookout Rd. At the intersection by the water treatment plant, turn left and drive about five miles until the road ends at Loch Lomond. From there, you're on your own!

◆3 Mt. McRae

When at Uncle Frank's Country Club (at the intersection of Highway 61 and 15th Side Road), look up at Mt. McRae and you'll see a prominent roof on a large round orange buttress. An incomplete route, (done in 2000?) by Jody Bernst and Shaun Parent goes up just to the left of the roof. It hasn't been cleaned and has no name. Bernst and Parent established a two-bolt anchor at the top of the cliff, and rapelled down 50 metres of the 100-metre wall, where they established another two-bolt anchor. They then climbed 50 metres of a sustained finger crack. Unfinished.

Lost Falls (see map opposite)

Route Character Sport – 2, Trad – 27, Mixed – 1, Toprope – 0, Multi-pitch – 3

Difficulty	5.8–	13
	5.9	3
	5.10	13
	5.11+	1

Travel   Drive time – 15 min., Hiking time: 15 min.

Getting There: Follow Highway 11/17 to the west side of Thunder Bay to Arthur Street. Continue southwest on Highway 61 (towards the U.S. border) for 12 km (past the Hwy 11/17 – Arthur Street junction). You will pass by the Thunder Bay airport. Turn left (south) onto Mountain Road and proceed for 1.3 km. Then turn right (south) onto Coppin Road. Drive to the end of this road and park in the cul-de-sac on the right side of the turnaround (west), clear of any local traffic and the adjacent driveways.

Lost Falls was established as an ice climb (3+) in 1985. While climbing there on a warm day in the Spring of 1998, Jon Balabuck, Chris Chapman & Jeff Hammerich came to realize the rock climbing potential of the area. They came back a few weeks later and claimed many of the first ascents listed here. Dave Benton, Will Meinen, J. Bamfield and Brandon Pullan spent more time here in 2001. There are still many potential routes here, especially on Big Thunder Wall.

Lost Falls is situated on Crown land and there are presently no access problems. However, make sure when parking at the end of Coppin Road, that your vehicle is not blocking any of the local residents' driveways.

Lost Falls is an area of mostly steep to vertical routes, especially crack routes, and large ledges. The area is very scenic. Given the undeveloped trail, you'll usually have to bushwhack a bit to find it. The face gets later afternoon and evening sun.

On the east side of the road there is a snowmobile/hiking trail. Follow this rough trail for 2 km trending to the southeast. At the first trail junction, stay right. At the second junction, turn left just after a short hill. Hike for about 500 metres to a flagged trail on the right hand side. (It may be hard to find; bushwhacking may be necessary). Hike through the forest and talus field, gradually rising, towards a box-shaped gap in the cliffs. The first climbs encountered (if you are on the trail) are at "The Little Block of Horrors."

Camping
The only available camp is a bivouac site on top of the cliffs.

Bouldering
On the trail into Lost Falls just before you enter the trees, there is a large boulder the size of a house on your right 10 metres into the trees. It's called the Bee Hive. There are five established boulder problems on it.

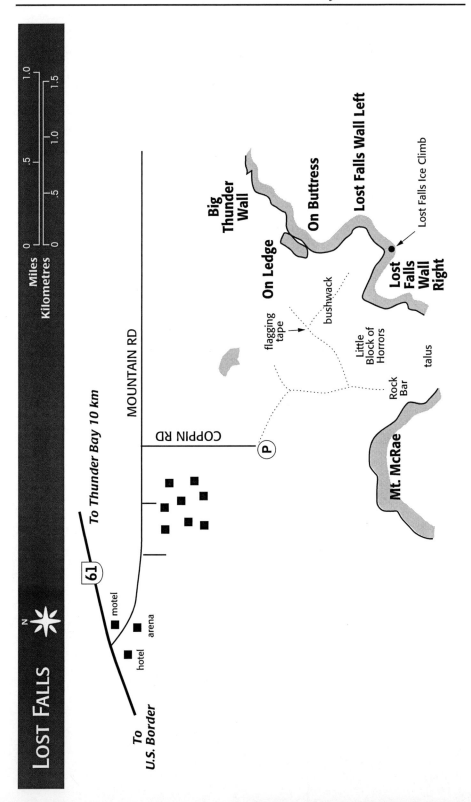

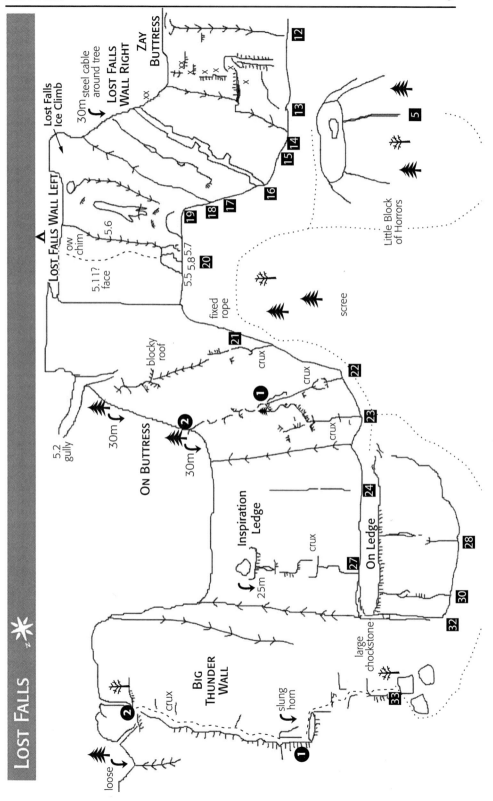

1 **Bumble Bugs**   V3

On the front face, near the tree that is very close to the boulder. Around the back side are:

2 **Boo Bees**   V1

3 **Honey, Nuts and Oats**   V4

4 **Num Nuts**   V1

This route is on a boulder on the right, just after leaving the trail to start the talus approach.

ALEX JOSEPH

Texas Chainsaw Massacre, 5.10a.

5 **Bam Bam**   10 Metres   5.9

Follow the zig zagging crack through the large boulder. Perfect your smearing techniques along the way. May have been done some time in the past. FA: Steven Gale, Brandon Pullan, March 2003.

Little Block of Horrors

The Little Block of Horrors is above the talus and on the right as you enter the bush, just before the main walls.

6 **Texas Chainsaw Massacre**   7 Metres   5.10a

Climb the short and slightly overhanging, rattly fist crack. Follow to the top and belay from a slung block. Find a key hold near the top. Looks easier than it is! Takes big gear, to #3 and #4 Camalots. FA: Jeff Hammerich, Tim Oliver, 1998.

7 **Poltergeist**   5 Metres   5.11

This climb follows a thin seam (which takes small nuts) with technical face climbing on small holds, up to a large crack. FA: J. Hammerich, 1998

8 **Casper**   3 Metres   V0

This is a great boulder problem up the razor sharp crack and onto the slab. FA: J. Hammerich, 1998.

The Rock Bar

In the fall of 2005, Will Meinen and Jason Bryant thrashed their way to the far western end of the Lost Falls area and found The Rock Bar, on the same band of rock as Lost Falls, far to the right (see map for location). The entire area is composed of quality rock from top to bottom, and riddled with cracks to solve. There is plenty of room here for continued development!

Routes are described from right to left. The first two climbs are located, side by side, on a small buttress at the far right of the crag.

9 **Beer for My Horses**   5.6

Follow the blocky crack system on the right side of the "mini buttress" to the bolted anchor at the top. FA: W. Meinen, J. Bryant, Fall 2005.

ALEX JOSEPH

MICHELLE SPIKOWSKI

On Buttress (L) and Zay Buttress.

10 Whiskey for My Men

5.8 ★★

Follow the crack system on the left side of the "mini buttress" through a flaring chimney with a hand crack tucked in the back. Rappel off of the bolt anchor. FA: J. Bryant, W. Meinen, Fall 2005.

11 First Round's on Me

5.8 ★★

Follow the continuous crack that starts in the obvious flaring corner. After working through the small overhang, power onto the face, and to the top. You'll want gear to 5". Rappel off of the slung tree. FA: J. Bryant, W. Meinen, Fall 2005.

Brandon Pullan on the FFA of Shinanigans.

12 Hard Day's Work   5.7

Climb the crack system, work around the chockstone, and trend right. Once under the roof, traverse left, then exit using the obvious crack. Or bring bigger gear and lay back the easy, but committing, off-width. Have some spare webbing, to replace one sling when you rappel off of the tree. FA: W. Meinen, J. Bryant, Fall 2005.

Zay Buttress

Formerly known as "Fly Buttress," this cliff is at the far south, right around the corner of Lost Falls Right wall and the off-width crack of "Too Tall for Webster." Routes are listed from right to left.

ALEX JOSEPH

Deceptacon and Too Tall for Webster, on Lost Falls Wall Right Side.

13 Idilly Bidilly   25 Metres   5.8

Start on the crack beside the bolts of "Shinanagans" and work up with a series of awkward jams. Cruise the middle and top section using the many blocky holds. This route still needs cleaning, and the top is a little loose. Takes gear to 3". FA: B. Pullan, May 2003.

14 Shinanigans   20 Metres   5.10–   ★★

The first sport route at Lost Falls. Six bolts. After a tricky first section, the route eases through moderate laybacks and flakes. The last moves hold a few surprises — take advantage of the oversized crimpers and fight that pump! There are two bolts at the top anchor. FA: B. Pullan, W. Mienen, April 2003. FFA: B. Pullan.

15 Hazey Waves   15 Metres   5.10c   ★★★

The arête left of Shinanagans now has eight bolts and a set of top anchors, marking a fun, juggy section with an airy crux sequence. Get that hazey, wavy feeling when you find you have no feet to use. There's an easy finish on the top of this fun route. FA: B. Pullan; FFA: B. Pullan, N. Gingrich, June 2004.

16 Crossing the Nile   15 Metres   5.10d   ★★★

Take on the thin, nice finger crack with no feet, left of the roof, and then traverse into Hazey Waves. Have some gear up to 1" to supplement the five bolts. Awkward and balancy, there's no other route like it in the area. FA: B. Pullan; FFA: B. Pullan, N. Gingrich, August 2004.

RANDY REED

Rene Lebel seconds Deceptacon.

Lost Falls Wall, Right Side

This wall is identified by a large corner on the left, which forms the "Lost Falls" ice climbing route (WI 3+) in the winter. Routes are listed from right to left.

17 Too Tall for Webster

45 Metres   5.9   ★★

This off-width route follows the massive jagged crack near the corner. FA: C. Chapman, J. Hammerich, J. Balabuck, 1998

18 Deceptacon

30 Metres   5.10   ★★

This prominent splitter crack line looks like a beauty and should be easy. It ain't. FA: C. Chapman, J. Hammerich, 1998.

ALEX JOSEPH

"Oh Shit..." follows the angled crack to the right of the birch tree.

FRANK PIANKA

Jenn Chikoski on Green Lantern, 5.8, Lost Falls Wall Right.

19 Green Lantern   *(see photo p. 8)*

40 Metres   5.8   ★ ★

FA: C. Chapman, J. Hammerich, J. Balabuck, 1998

Lost Falls Wall, Left Side

20 O Shit I'm Dead and My Arm's Real Long 25 Metres 5.8

Follow the crack and face directly left of the Lost Falls ice climb. Named after the strange water-mark figure left on wall half way up. Needs gear to 2".

21 Escape from the Black Flies 25 Metres 5.5–5.8

Start left on blocky talus and climb to the large ledge, and then up a gully/chimney through the top (5.5). Or start in the middle, in the finger crack behind a birch tree that leads to same large ledge. Then follow the same chimney/gully to the top (5.8+). Or try your luck at the overhanging face (5.11?). Or start in the right crack…work to same large ledge and up (5.7). All these variations are still dirty with loose rock on most ledges. Leaders need gear to 4", or this route will take a toprope with 10-12 metres of webbing for the anchors. FA: B. Pullan, Michelle Spakowski, June 2003.

On Buttress

This cliff is on the south face (north side) of the talus area, to the left of the Lost Falls ice route. Routes are listed right to left.

22 Copper's Breakfast 30 Metres 5.7 ★

Works well as a two pitch route. Pitch 1—a short challenging climb to the ledge, then (pitch 2) go long for the top. A fun route on a great line. FA: J. Bamfield, B. Pullan, 2001

23 Priority Check (2 pitches) 50 Metres 5.8+ ★ ★

Pitch 1: Follow the super fun crack climb to a spacious belay. Pitch 2: Have a fine time wandering up solid rock to the top. FA: W. Meinen, Dave Benton, 2001.

24 Danebat (see photo p. 12) 15 Metres 5.10d ★ ★ ★

A harder first pitch to "Priority Check." Work up the stiff overhanging crack cleaned by Chris Chapman. Go up to a ledge and right (precarious but safe) to meet up with "Priority Check" just before the first belay. FA: D. Benton, W. Meinen, 2001.

On Ledge

These four routes start from the ledge just left and around the corner north of "Danebat."

25 Anchors Away 30 Metres 5.9, A1

A crack route, and kind of blocky. A little dirty but fun. FA: B. Pullan, May 2003.

NICK BUDA

26 Cinnamon
25 Metres   5.10c

Climb the first half of
"Anchors Away" past
the fixed nut, then con-
tinue straight up instead
of taking the right
crack. Fun and a little
dirty. Gear to 2." FA: B.
Pullan; FFA: B. Pullan,
N. Gingrich, July 2004.

27 Scoliosis
5.10a   20 Metres

Patrick Martel about to go airborne on Danebat.

Climb the huge curving crack 5 metres right of "Foxy" into the dirty dihedral to the
Leaning Pillar Ledge. Bring a brush! Needs gear to 3." The only good descent is to rap
off. FA: B. Pullan; FFA: B. Pullan, N. Gingrich, June, 2004.

28 Foxy   5.10a   25 Metres   ★ ★

This is the fine-looking finger crack that starts from a wicked viewpoint where the
ledge ends. Steep, varied, and sustained, this route has great moves above great gear.
Rappel from a webbing anchor on "Inspiration Ledge." Be sure to have webbing that
you can leave behind. FA: D. Benton, W. Meinen, 2001.

Will Meinen on the FA of Mother-Son Relations.

The next three climbs are on the lower-level cliff below the base of "Foxy."

29 Mr. Sandman

5.10a   12m   ★ ★

Climb the shallow corner crack right of "Mother-Son Relations" to a birch tree. Use both walls to the sides. Takes small gear to 1/4," and small nuts. FA: B. Pullan; FFA: B. Pullan, N. Gingrich, July, 2004.

30 Mother-Son Relations

20 Metres?   5.9   ★ ★

A cruxy roof leads to a lengthy off-width/fist crack. Fun – if you like that sort of thing. Bring a 4" cam! FA: W. Meinen, D. Benton, 2001.

31 Sandbag 20 Metres?   5.10b

 ★ ★ 🛍

A stout (harder than 5.10b) bouldery start leads to a killer layback crack! This pitch could be combined with "Foxy" to make a two-pitch 5.10. FA: D. Benton, W. Meinen, 2001

32 Minding Margaret

20 metres   5.10b

Start right of "No Fat People," traverse the horizontal finger crack right around the corner and up the dihedral. FA: Shawn Robinson; FFA: Shawn Robinson, July 8, 2004.

33 No Fat People

15 Metres?   5.5   ★

This route is a squeeze chimney with good gear; great for eager beginners. Wedge your way up this rather large crevasse with a large chockstone near the top, at the base of "Foxy."
FA: W. Meinen, D. Benton, 2001.

Will Meinen the FA of No Fat People, 5.5.

Big Thunder Wall

This is the large west-facing wall that faces the old "Big Thunder" ski jumping facility across the valley to the west. It is around the corner left (north) of "Foxy."

34 Myopic Adventure

(2–3 pitches) 45 Metres 5.8

 ★ ★

Look north beyond the great stance at the base of "Foxy," around to the most obvious right-facing dihedral and its orange lichen-covered line. This route may still require some cleaning as the first ascent was done ground-up. Take gear to 3+". Variations of both the first and second pitch have been done, and are described below. They all use the same second pitch belay.

Derrik Patola and Nick Buda on pitch two of Myopic Adventure, 5.8.

Pitch 1: Scramble up to a set of birch trees in a corner. Climb up, and then trend left and up the cracked corner, to eventually reach a big ledge. Move left into the corner for a gear and slung rock belay (5.4, 15 metres).

Pitch 2: Climb up the crack/dihedral system through some roofs. Dig deep in your technique for some incredible finger jams, stemming, and the odd face hold. The crux is the last move to reach a ledge with a large cedar tree, on the right. Belay here with large gear off the tree and escape south OR,

(Pitch 3) Continue up the five-metre fist crack on the left, to top out on a rubbly ledge with a pine tree (5.8, 30 metres). FFA (ground-up onsight): Alex Joseph, Jarron Childs, July 2002.

NICK BUDA

Jen Haink on Myopic Adventure Direct, 5.8+.

35 Myopic Adventure Direct

(alternate 1st pitch) 15 Metres 5.8+

 ★

Why scramble the first pitch? There's a perfect left-facing hand crack that splits right up the lower wall to the base of the second pitch. FFA: Shawn Robinson, Andy Gallant, April 17, 2004.

36 Myopic Adventure Face

(alternate 2nd pitch) 20 Metres 5.10

Just right of original second pitch, from the first belay work the thin, poorly-protected face on suspect holds and dubious small cams. A very reachy crux leads to a good rest, then to a 5.7 crack that joins the original route at the end of its second pitch. Not recommended; FFA: Jan Hank, Nick Buda May 29, 2004.

ALEX JOSEPH

Jarron Childs seconding Alex Joseph on the FFA of Myopic Adventure, 5.8.

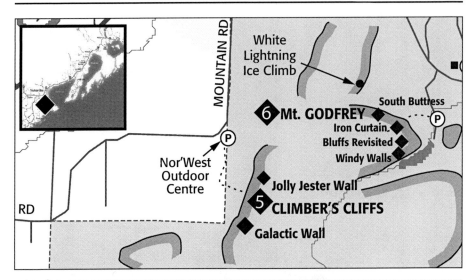

5 ⬥ Climbers Cliffs

Route Character Sport – 4, Trad – 17, Mixed – 8, Toprope – 1, Multi-pitch – 3

Difficulty	
5.8–	12
5.9	7
5.10	6
5.11+	3

Travel   Drive time – 15 min., Hiking time – 15 min.

Getting There: From the Harbour Expressway follow Highway 11/17 west to Highway 61, heading south towards the American border. Take Highway 61 for 8.5 km and turn left onto Chippewa Road, following it to Mountain Road. At Pelletier's gas station turn right, (that is, stay on Mountain Road) and go over two hills. From the top of the second hill the cliffs can be seen up in the distance. Continue along Mountain Road for 2.3 km (from Chippewa Road) and look for the Nor'west Outdoor Centre. (Watch for their sign on a sharp corner). Pull into the driveway and park in the lot. Well-established trails go approximately one km through the woods to the cliff.

One of the trails leads you to Jolly Jester Wall first, and the other branch of the trail leads you to the Sickle Wall area. A trail runs along the cliffs connecting all areas.

This is an area of steep to vertica l routes, with ledges and enjoyable crack lines, great gear leads, maintained sport routes and bouldering. The good quality diabase cliffs here max out at just over 50 metres. The area is home to many excellent routes, both traditional and bolted. There are also a number of established bouldering problems within the talus field. The trails and to a certain extent the climbs are more often climbed and maintained than some other areas. The exposure is such that the crags get late afternoon and evening sun.

This area is on land that is now owned by the Nor'west Outdoor Centre. They allow access to these cliffs on days when they are not being used for the Centre's clients.

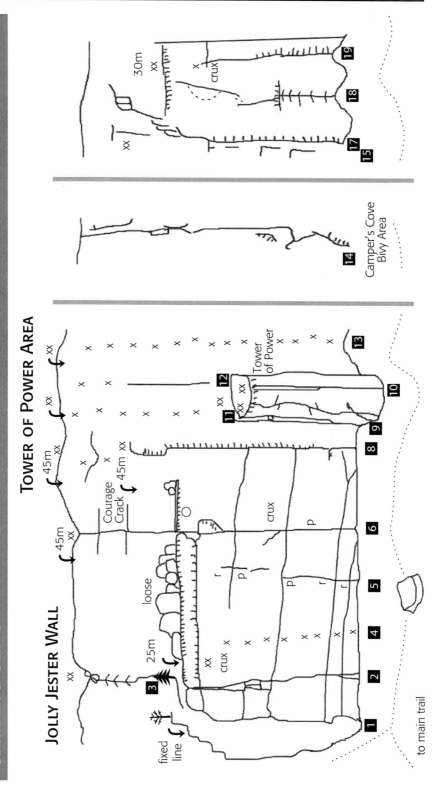

CLIMBER'S CLIFFS

TOWER OF POWER AREA

JOLLY JESTER WALL

Courage Crack

loose

fixed line

to main trail

Tower of Power

Camper's Cove Bivy Area

CLIMBER'S CLIFFS

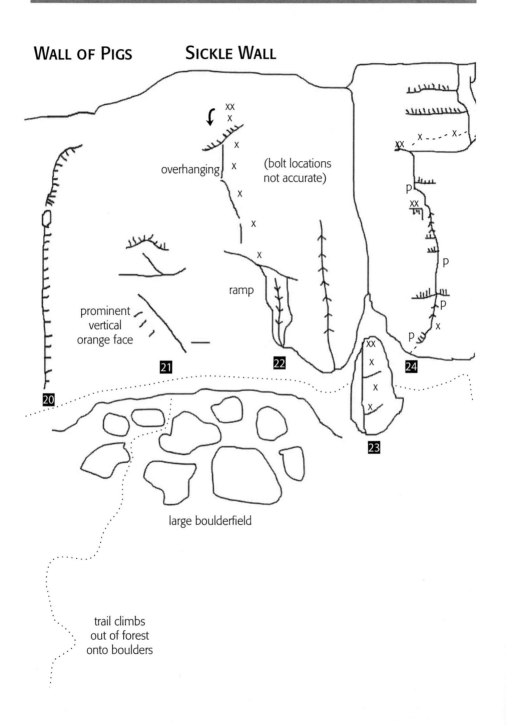

WALL OF PIGS   **SICKLE WALL**

overhanging

(bolt locations not accurate)

ramp

prominent vertical orange face

large boulderfield

trail climbs out of forest onto boulders

Climber's Cliffs

Location: These routes are all right of routes on p. 18

Windalogo Wall

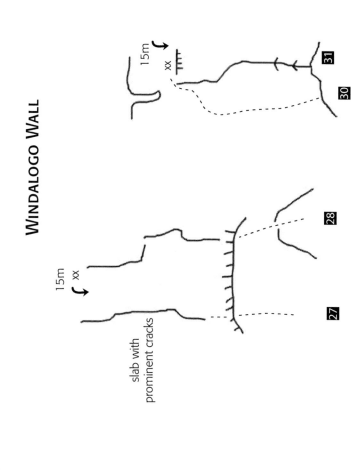

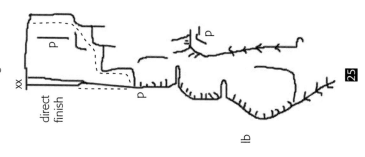

You MUST phone (807) 475-8346 well in advance of climbing here, in order to arrange a meeting to sign legal waivers and to assure that you and students are not in each others' way. The Chapmans will then provide information on trails. They can also provide information on route development in the area.

This area was originally discovered over two decades ago when Shaun Parent and friends did a few of the more obvious (but not necessarily aesthetically pleasing) lines, and also worked the Jolly Jester wall. Further development of this crag occurred when Chris Chapman, Jeff Hammerich and others freed a number of aid routes, climbed some new cracks, and bolted what may become the first 5.13a in the region, "Electric Gigolo."

Jolly Jester Wall

This is the most northern (left) wall at Climbers Cliffs.

1 Den
25 Metres 5.7

Start next to the birch below the white pine tree with rap slings that is the top of this route. Go up under the roof, then jam up the crack and curve right to a slightly over-hanging fist and arm flake. FA: G. Lauziere, S. Parent, 1979.

2 Tudy
25 Metres   5.8

★★

This is one of the area's off-width test pieces. Start left of the bolted blank face of "Electric Gigolo." Climb up the obvious fist/off-width crack on the left side of the face, using some small ledges, to the tree. The last move is a full-on off-width chimney. Use the fixed line descent to the north, or climb "Bushed" (not recommended) above to the top. Needs gear to 4+". FA: S. Parent, G. Lauziere, 1979.

Shaun Parent on the FA of Tudy.

Randy Reed does Tudy.

3 Bushed (2nd pitch)   15 Metres   5.6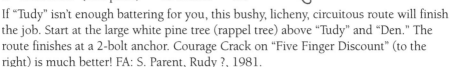

If "Tudy" isn't enough battering for you, this bushy, licheny, circuitous route will finish the job. Start at the large white pine tree (rappel tree) above "Tudy" and "Den." The route finishes at a 2-bolt anchor. Courage Crack on "Five Finger Discount" (to the right) is much better! FA: S. Parent, Rudy ?, 1981.

4 Electric Gigolo   22 Metres   5.13a?   ★★

This is a still-incomplete project that will likely prove to be the first 5.13 in the region. Levitate the wide blank face north of "Five Finger Discount." Difficult, reachy moves at the start lead to improbable moves to finish on the steepening, deteriorating slab at a pair of fixed anchors just below the large blocky ledge. Eight bolts. FA: S. Parent [tr]. 1982? (Jolly Jester Wall) FA: J. Hammerich, C. Chapman, 1999. FFA: J. Hammerich, C. Chapman to near the top (5.12+?)

5 Blade Runner   22 Metres   A2+

This route follows the thin blade crack running up the face to the left of "Five Finger Discount." There are two fixed pieces above the high point that Dedi and Parent recorded in the original guide to the area. Takes gear to 1.5," a standard nailing rack, extra blades, bashies, bat hooks, and two pins. There are/were three fixed copperheads. This route was used as the A3 test route for the only ORCA Instructor Evaluation course ever offered in the Thunder Bay area. FA: S. Parent. New high point: Randy Reed (solo), October 1997.

Shaun Parent on the FA of Five Finger Discount, 5.8.

6 Five Finger Discount
45 Metres   5.8

 ★ ★ ★

This classic pitch is the most often climbed route in the area. Originally graded 5.7, it has fine, varied moves and excellent protection. The lower portion offers few easy moves, using finger jams and face holds through bomber hand holds past an old piton. Continue through great moves to the ledge. Belay off of gear here, or continue up "Courage Crack" (5.6) another 20 metres, as the angle eases a bit. Descent: A second line allows a full rappel, or rappel 20 metres to the belay ledge and scramble along the ledge to the rappel (25 metres) above "Tudy." Gear to 3." FA: S. Parent, P. Dedi, 1981.

7 Horizontal Wastelands   V0

Traverse between "Five Finger Discount" and "Tudy" along the slanting, nearly horizontal crack about 2 metres off the ground. FA: S. Parent, Joanne Murphy-Parent, 1982.

8 Wet Dreams

(2 pitches)   45 Metres   5.8+

 ★ ★

Right of "Five Finger Discount" and 10 metres left (north) of the "Tower of Power" is a dihedral, which looks a little dirty and is sometimes wet. Climb the corner following several wide hand or thin fist cracks almost straight up to a ledge with bolt anchors. The second pitch continues up the overhanging section, which has two bolts. Follow the easiest line through this roof up onto a ledge with a shrub. Top out on two rappel anchors. Have lots of big gear to 4" with double 2"-3" pieces. FA (1st pitch): P. Dedi, S. Parent (5.4, A2). FFA: Jody Bernst, C. Chapman (bolts to the top), 1997.

Rappelling down along Wet Dreams.

Tower of Power Area

There are two routes on the Tower itself, which end at a two-bolt anchor fixed in the top of the tower. There is a rappel anchor five metres to the right of the finish to "Bong It In." Two other routes climb the wall above the Tower.

9 Bong It In *(see photo in color section)*

20 Metres   5.10a   ★ ★

This slightly overhanging jagged crack is on the north face of the Tower. A fixed stopper is near the top. Stem the chimney between the pillar and the large block, then climb a hand and finger crack to the top of the pillar and a two bolt anchor. FA: S. Parent (5.7 A2, 45 Metres?) FFA: J. Bernst, C. Chapman, 1997.

NICK BUDA

Shawn Robinson coming up Snake Skin, 5.9.

10 Thick and Thin
20 Metres   5.9

 ★

This thin crack, which opens up to a full off-width, is three metres right of "Bong It In" on the west face of the Tower of Power. Though there are bolts, have gear to 4-5." FA: C. Chapman, Spring 1999.

11 Snake Skin
(2nd pitch)
15 Metres   5.9

 ★

This is the sport route on the left that starts on top of the Tower of Power. Follow the bolts, staying left at the top. 6 bolts. FA: J. Bernst, C. Chapman, 1997.

12 Hot Plate
(2nd pitch)
20 Metres   5.10b R

 ★

This mixed route starts on top of the Tower of Power, a couple of metres to the right of "Snake Skin." The seam leads up to two bolts, and finally to a 2-bolt rappel station. Take a standard rack, with gear to 2." FA: J. Bernst, C. Chapman, 1997.

13 Fit To Be Tied   40 Metres   5.11b   ★★

Up and right from the Tower of Power, scramble up to the base of the face just left of a large dirty corner. A hard start leads to sustained face climbing. 14 bolts. FA: J. Bernst, C. Chapman, 1997.

14 Fashion and Accessories   45 Metres   5.7

Above and slightly to the right of the bivi cave (Camper's Cove), this route goes up the right side of the big orange buttress. You'll find the cave when following along the cliff north (left) after the main trail arrives at the cliff. FA: P. Dedi, Bob Porter, 1982.

15 Jeff's Joke   17 Metres   5.7

Not a lot of fun, this route and "Jeff's Second Joke" (below) are set up primarily for the climbing school. A permanent line is set up through the chains for rigging a toprope.

Just left of "Jeff's 2nd Joke," climb the face to a ledge with chains. FA: J. Hammerich, C. Chapman.

16 Jeff's Second Joke   17 Metres   5.7

Just left of "Lauziere Chimney," climb the face to a ledge with chains just below the top of the chimney. FA: J. Hammerich, C. Chapman.

17 Lauziere Chimney   50 Metres   5.4

This distinctive squeeze chimney line is in the back of a large left-facing corner, uphill and right (south) right of the Camper's Cove bivy cave. Finish by scrambling up blocky ledges. FA: S. Parent, G. Lauziere, 1979.

18 Fuck It   40 Metres   C3   ★★

Just around the corner (right) of Lauziere Chimney, an excellent dihedral/corner climbs up to a quickdraw hanging from the roof. Then, traverse left through the roof, and work up a hand crack to some sketchy hooking, heading left across the face past a fixed natural thread to the two-bolt belay on the ledge directly above "Cobra In the Kindergarten." Take a good assortment of hooks and RP's. Don't bother topping out. Unrepeated to date. FA: R. Reed, Todd Free, 1999.

NICK BUDA

Mark Powell on the FA of Cobra in the Kindergarten, 5.10.

19 Cobra In the Kindergarten   30 Metres   5.10   ★

This beautiful finger crack is in a left-facing corner just right of "Fuck It." Work up the crack to a finish on bolts. Crux is at the top. Take a standard rack to supplement the three or four bolts. FA: Mark Powell, Stacey Schrattner, 2003.

Wall of Pigs

This route is 150 metres right (south) of "Fuck It."

20 Death Wish Chimney   40 Metres   5.8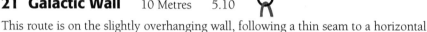

This line is easily identified as the widest, loosest, most dangerous-looking chimney around. Working past the freezer-sized chockstone near top is the crux. FA: S. Parent, G. Lauziere, 1979.

Sickle Wall

This area is identified by the most solid rock in the middle of the cliff with a very short (10–15 metres) left-trending diagonal line starting at the right hand edge of the talus slope.

21 Galactic Wall   10 Metres   5.10

This route is on the slightly overhanging wall, following a thin seam to a horizontal crack. FA: Paul Mahoney, 1982.

22 Arrested For Mopery   20 Metres   5.12, A0   ★ ★

This slightly overhanging wall starts with a number of very thin moves up a ramp (the sling that was placed to protect the red point attempt may be needed to overcome the first move) to a mainly bomber face crack that is harder than it looks. Things get cruxy after the fourth bolt. Top anchors and seven bolts. FA: C. Chapman, J. Hammerich FFA: not completed to date?

23 Stiffy   5 Metres   5.10-   ★

In the gully between "Galactic Wall" and "Uncle Frank's Supper Club," this short route is on the southwest of a small detached pinnacle. Climb through two horizontal ledges just left of the arête. A good warm up for "Arrested For Mopery." There is a sling rappel anchor on top. Three bolts. FA: J. Hammerich, Fall 1999.

SHAUN PARENT COLLECTION

Shaun Parent on the FA of
Uncle Frank's Supper Club, 5.7 A2.

24 Uncle Frank's Supper Club
45 Metres   5.10+ (5.7, A2)   ★ ★

Start on the far right side of talus pile. Climb with small wires or rurps past several fixed pins to the substantial ledge. Follow a knife blade crack in the dihedral to a second ledge below a roof, which has another pin. Pull through the roof to a pair of bolts on the ledge above. Rappel, or traverse right across the ledge to climb a dirty finish (5.7) out near the nose. FA: S. Parent, Linn Jones, P. Dedi, 1983. FFA: J. Bernst, J. Hammerich, C. Chapman (onsight), 1998.

25 Ignorance & Arrogance   40 Metres   5.9   ★★

This substantial left-facing dihedral/crack route is 20 metres to the right and around the corner from "Uncle Frank's." Climb the corner and layback up the big flakes. Traverse right along ledges and up blocks to the top. A direct (and better) finish goes at 5.9, straight up from the first ledge into the off-width. There is a two-bolt rappel anchor at the top of the off-width. Have a #4 or #5 Camalot for the off-width varation. FA: P. Dedi, D. Pugliese, 1982. FA (direct finish): C. Chapman, 1998.

26 Ball Buster   40 Metres   A2

This route takes the big loose dihedral 20 metres to the right of "Ignorance and Arrogance." Continue diagonally left to the crack near the top. FA: C. Chapman, J. Hammerich, 1997.

Windalogo Wall

27 Feature Presentation   18 Metres   5.10 R   ★★

The lower part of this small wall has solid rock and some fine routes. Solve the over-hanging start and then continue up on a less-than-vertical face. There are two bolts off of the start. The slab above has some substantial runout. There are variations here graded as hard as 5.10d/11a. Have a standard rack to go with the two bolts. FA: C. Chapman.

28 Sneak Preview   18 Metres   5.9   ★★

Another overhanging start moves into a fine crack line up the slab. Beautiful trad placements on the route lead to a pair of bolts for top anchors. FA: J. Hammerich.

29 ACO   15 Metres   5.8   ★

About 30 metres beyond "Sneak Preview" and just right of a sizable slab, this system of cracks is tucked away in a corner. The upper level is pretty messy, so there's a rappel station at the top of the route. FA: Alpine Club Outing. Cleaned by C. Chapman.

Approximately 30 metres further to the right (south) of "ACO" (that is, 60 metres from 'Sneak Preview") are two short climbs before the access gully to the top of the cliff.

30 Easter Surprise   10 Metres   5.7   ★

Climb only the face to the left of "Identity Crisis." End at the same two-bolt anchor. FA: J. Hammerich '98.

31 Identity Crisis   10 Metres   5.9   ★

Follow the corner/crack system up to the vertical face and pop up onto the horizontal block, to a 2-bolt rappel anchor. FA: C. Chapman, 1998.

32 Black Plague   9 Metres   5.9

This short but sweet line is 15 metres further right (south) of "Easter Surprise" and just left of the access gully. Proceed up the layback crack to a short, overhanging finger crack. This climb was first climbed ground up, onsight. Rappel into the gully from slings on the tree. FFA: (onsight) J. Hammerich, C. Chapman, 1998.

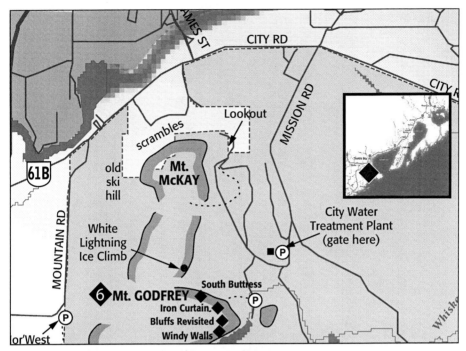

6 Mt. Godfrey

Route Character Sport – 5, Trad – 7, Mixed – 0, Toprope – 7, Multi-Pitch – 0

Difficulty		
5.8–	4
5.9	1
5.10	8
5.11+	5

Travel Time   Drive time – 30 min., Hike – 15 min.

Getting There: On Mission Road, south of Thunder Bay, turn right to go to the Mt. McKay Lookout, but once past the gate turn immediately left onto a dirt road. Take the right at the next fork in the road. At the end of the road there is a small clearing with three pine trees. On the city side (north), a trail marked in blue flagging tape takes you to the Iron Curtain and South Buttress areas. South Buttress, which has amazing views from the top, is undeveloped. The Iron Curtain is further up the road, which becomes a trail. To get to the top, continue along the trail until you get to a huge boulder, turn right off the trail and scramble up the talus slope to the left. Blue flagging tape and an old rope lead you to the top. Beware that some routes are longer than a full-length rope.

This north facing, shaded, cliff lies high above the city and has great views. The routes are steep to vertical, and so a number of the routes here were established as topropes and are still climbed that way. This is an area that is does not see a lot of climbers. It may be the vegetated approach deters people. That is unfortunate, as there is still lots of potential on these rarely climbed walls.

Access Issues

These cliffs are on aboriginal land. Maintaining a low profile and respecting their rights as landowners will help ensure that this beautiful area remains open.

History

Any ice climber will tell you that Godfrey abounds with long, hard route possibilities. Only 5 minutes south of the city, developed routes lie between "Ice Stud" to the south and "White Lightning" to the north. Shaun Bent and Bryce Brown spent the spring of 1996 developing the rock routes in this area.

Iron Curtain

Routes described from left to right. Deja Vu is left of the path to the top.

1 Deja Vu   10 Metres   5.9+

This route is on the front of the small buttress just to the left of the trail leading to the top. FA: S. Bent, Bryce Brown, 1996.

2 Eskimos Kiss   13 Metres   5.10b

Five bolts.

3 Bear Hug   12 Metres   5.10b   ★ ★ ★

This route, with four bolts, was originally established as "Gilligans Island," at 5.10a. Climb a sustained series of sloper holds to a nice hold at the top. FFA: B. Pullan.

4 Birch Out of Rock   10 Metres   5.7

Climb the obvious route with the small birch stump three-fourths of the way up. FA: S. Bent, Bryce Brown, 1996.

5 Stone Roses   13 Metres   5.10c

Just to the right of "Birch Out of Rock." This route requires some thought-provoking moves. FA: S. Bent, Bryce Brown, 1996.

6 The Fearless Blind Man   15 Metres   5.10–   ★

Climb the crack to the roof. Once over, traverse right to another crack and up to the top. FA: S. Bent, R. Dynes, 1996.

7 A.S.A.   9 Metres   5.8   ★

Climb the series of cracks and seams to the top. FA: S. Bent, Bryce Brown, 1996.

8 Tamarack   22 Metres   5.12b/c   ★ ★

Start on "The Whipping," then head right onto new ground before moving left to finish on easy holds. The crux is the middle section near the sixth bolt. Very reachy and balancy, and the grade is height dependent. 10 bolts, and top anchors. FA: B. Pullan; FFA: B. Pullan, S. Gale.

MT. GODFREY

IRON CURTAIN

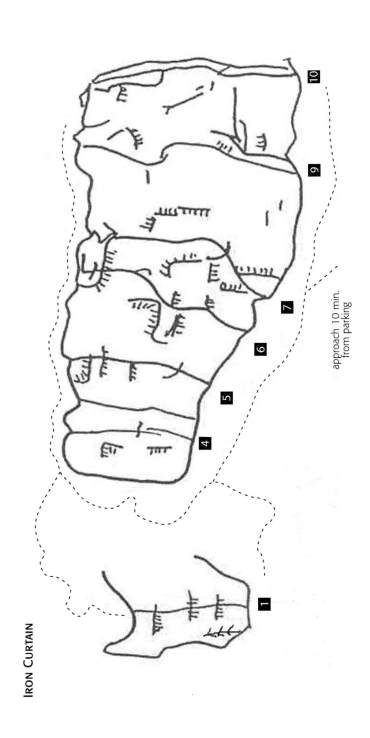

approach 10 min.
from parking

Windy Walls

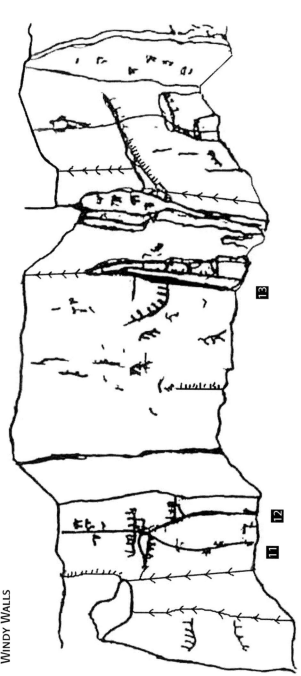

Windy Walls with Lost Traditions. The prominent chimney is Spearhead Chimney, with Echoes of the Totem just to its right.

9 The Whipping   22 Metres   5.11b   ★

Climb out from the roof to a series of ledges, then to the steep crux section and finally to a very balancy finish. A 0.5" cam and lots of webbing helps for setting up the toprope. One bolt on top. FA: S. Bent, Bryce Brown, 1996.

10 Renaissance Man   22 Metres   5.11d   ★

Just left of the roof, proceed up an easy start to the very thin and balancy crux. FA: S. Bent, 1996.

Windy Walls

Routes are described from left (east) to right (west).

11 Chemically High   30 Metres   5.10b

Start just to the left of "Dynamic Duo." Climb the face to the ledge two-thirds of the way up, and finish on "Dynamic Duo." FA: S. Bent, Bryce Brown, 1996.

12 Dynamic Duo   30 Metres   5.11a

Climb the crack that starts 10 feet off the ground to a ledge two-thirds of the way up, then negotiate the roof and crack to the top. FA: S. Bent, Bryce Brown, 1996.

13 'Shrooming Experience   27 Metres   5.8+

Start on a large ledge, and climb up series of small ledges to a corner. Finish up the open book crux. FA: S. Bent, Bryce Brown, 1996.

14 Unknown   27 Metres   5.10a

Scramble up to a large ledge to the start, then up the slab to the roof and an overhanging finish.

Ol' West Area

This wall is 20 metres left of "Dynamic Duo."

15 The Wrangler   22 Metres   5.12b    ★ ★ ★

This is a route with a bit of everything. Thin technical face moves to start, then some nice laybacks to crimpy side pulls with a heel hook. With feet on nothing, throw for the jug. Then move to the balancy slab that's a lot like Squamish, and hit the face with a 65 degree roof and technical moves above it. Work up the arête and into the dihedral. 10 bolts, with anchors at the top. FA: B Pullan, Steve Gale ; FFA: Jason Thorne, Sept. 2004.

16 Lost Traditions (2 Pitches)   30 Metres   5.10b   ★ ★

Take on the clean fist crack to the belay. Stick right up and under the roof with good feet and into the roof. Take the face to the top. Gear to 4." FA: B. Pullan; FFA: B. Pullan, S. Gale, Fall 2004.

17 Right of Way (2 Pitches)   30 Metres   5.10+   ★ ★ ★

Start on the same first pitch as "Lost Traditions" and stay right up the nice dihedral crack. This route gets balancy and thin near the top. FA: B. Pullan; FFA: B. Pullan, S. Gale, Fall 2004.

18 Spear Head Chimney   30 Metres   5.5

Up around the flakey slab, left of "Echoes of the Totem," This route is loose and dirty, but it is some crazy fun. FA: B. Pullan (solo), Summer 2004.

Totem Pole Area *(see photo in color section)*

BRANDON PULLAN

Echoes of the Totem, 5.12c/d

19 Echoes of the Totem
25 Metres   5.12c/d

 ★ ★ ★

On its own wall away from the main cliff, this climb is an adventure to be had. Work up the thin-looking overhanging wall, following a line of bolts. A tough first move (V4) gets you into a balancy section that runs till the fifth bolt. The next rest is at the eighth bolt, to allow you to prepare to lace together a series of awkward pulls and crimps to the anchors. Originally graded 5.13a, this line has since been downgraded by Jason Thorne. 12 bolts and top anchors. FA: Brandon Pullan, Steve Gale; FFA: Jason Thorne, Dave Hereema.

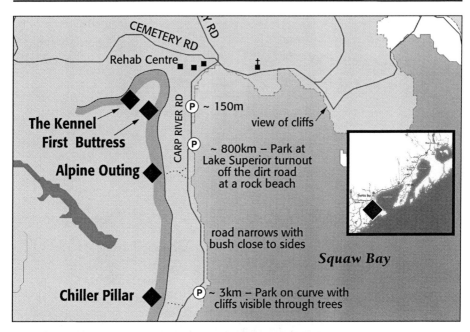

7 **Squaw Bay**

Route Character Sport – 5, Trad – 32, Mixed – 7, Toprope – 5, Multi-pitch – 15

Difficulty		
5.8	16	
5.9	7	
5.10	14	
5.11+	9	

Travel   Drive time – 30 min., Hiking time – 15 min.

Getting There: When driving into Thunder Bay from the south, Highway 61B exits right (south) off of Highway 61 and becomes City Road. In the city going south, Highway 61B winds around in the city until (as James Street) it crosses the Kaministiqua River, and intersects with City Road.

About one kilometre past the intersection of James Street and City Road, Mission Road turns right (south) and goes toward the Rehab Centre, The Kennel, First Buttress, Alpine Wall, and Chiller Pillar. To get to "The Wrinkles," continue on City Road about four kilometres past Mission Road, and park near or at the Chippewa Animal Park/Zoo.

There are four different cliff areas near Squaw Bay, and three overlook Lake Superior. The main area of development is on three sets of cliffs that stretch from Squaw Bay for approximately four kilometres along a dirt road. Another small outcrop of interesting rock (The Wrinkles) is located in the forest east of the main cliffs, on the other side of Squaw Bay.

Squaw Bay is an area to go for spectacular scenery and cool breezes. The lake also offers swimming, though the water never gets very warm. The cliff lines face east and southeast, so they get morning sun. The routes are mostly longer, on steep to vertical rock. Most were established on lead, involved significant cleaning, and have an alpine feel to them, including the possibility of loose rock. Belay stances should be planned accordingly. This is mainly a "ground up" area, with toproping limited to the little routes on "The Wrinkles." If you find a route that doesn't seem to be in the book, there's a reason; there is still substantial new route potential here.

These cliffs are located on aboriginal land. In order to keep this area open, keep a low profile. Drive slowly on the dirt roads, and avoid any impacts on the local environment. Stay on established trails when you find them, pack out your garbage and pick up others', and limit vegetation removal. These cliffs are also home to eagles and peregrine falcons which nest particularly on the "Alpine Outing" wall. Avoid this area during nesting season, from mid-June to the end of July.

The Wrinkles

Just past the Chippewa Animal Park/Zoo and across from mailbox 102, find the trail on right side of road and follow it for about 10 minutes. Persevere; the rock is not visible from the road and the brush is dense. Bring lots of webbing to set up the topropes.

1 Scrodumb   5 Metres   5.7
Climb the flakes to the left of the widening crack. FA: Mike O'Brien and friends.

2 After the Goldrush   7 Metres   5.10–   ★
Climb the face to the left of the arête, following right of the undercling flake and between the parallel vertical cracks. A #4 Camalot helps to set up the toprope on this climb. FA: M. O'Brien and friends.

3 Jackson's Climb   7 Metres   5.9   ★
Climb up the right side of the crack in the middle of the face, next to the stump. There are bolts for a top anchor. FA: M. O'Brien, C. Jackson and friends.

4 Wrinkles Direct   7 Metres   5.7   ★
Climb the face to the right of the corner, just above where the trail meets the cliff. Two #3 Camalots help on the toprope setup of this climb. FA: Mike O'Brien and friends.

5 Unknown   8 Metres   5.9   ★
This route is around the other side of the detached cliff block from "Jackson's Climb" and nearly opposite "Wrinkles Direct." FA: Unknown.

The Kennel

This west-facing bluff, tucked in behind the Alcohol Rehab Centre, is huge and has a lot of potential. Park far off on the edge of the road, near the end of the Rehab Center driveway. There is a newly-cut trail leading up and west through talus and loose rock directly to the base of the cliff. (Ice climbers will recognize this as the area just left of the ice climbs "Wet Ones" and "Rainy Day Woman.") This area needs a little more traffic and maybe a bit more cleaning, but it's worth the work.

Descent: There's a good clean rappel from the top of "Dark Dog" all the way to the bottom, if you have double ropes.

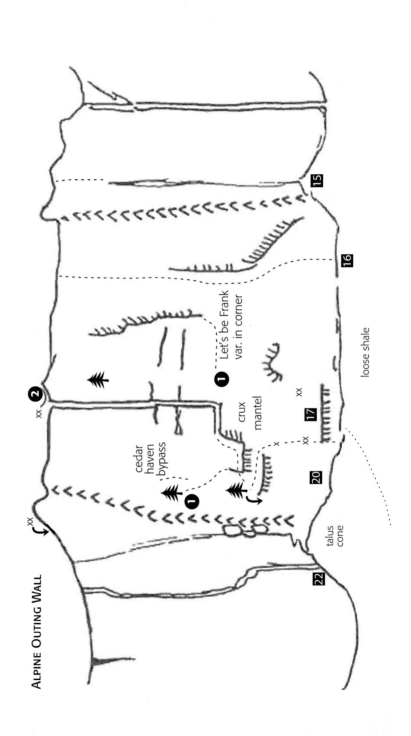

SQUAW BAY

ALPINE OUTING WALL

cedar
haven
bypass

crux
mantel

Let's be Frank
var. in corner

loose shale

talus
cone

15

16

17

20

22

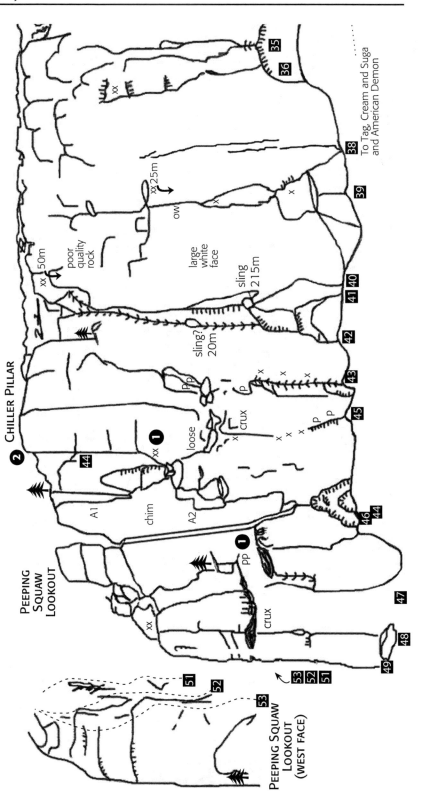

The Kennel – all this rock and only four established routes.

6 **Shin Breaker Gully**   60 Metres   III   Scramble

30 metres right of "Mad Dog," climb the ever-steepening gully. Fun and loose.
FA: B. Pullan, D. Patola, Summer 2004.

7 **Mad Dog** (1 or 2 Pitches)   35 Metres   5.10    ★ ★ ★

This is a pleasant route, even though it's an off-width. Pitch 1: Start to the left of the
large block with a tree on it. Climb to the slung block and belay from there. Pitch 2:
Head straight up the stellar crack to an off-width and then over the small roof to a nice
ledge. Have gear up to 5" for the second pitch. FFA: Brandon Pullan, Derek Patola,
Fall 2004.

8 **Kat Scratch**   55 metres   5.10

Climb the sustained and continuous crack, several hundred feet to the right of Dark
Dog. Bring big gear, up to a #3.5 Camalot. The easiest descent is to rappel from the
bolts at the top of Dark Dog. FA: W. Meinen, J.Bryant, Fall 2005.

9 **Dark Dog** (2 Pitches)   45 Metres   5.8+    ★ ★ ★

This is two pitches of classic granite climbing. Pitch 1: Start on a bit of loose rock and
get up into the crack under the roof. Climb the layback crack to the roof, protecting
with large gear, and reach high above, hanging on a jam, while your body is parallel to
the ground. Grab the "Thank God" hold and pull up and over on huge jugs. Above the
roof, place protection to the left in a horizontal crack, as it's easy to get your rope
caught in the crack. Keep gear to belay on the ledge. Pitch 2: Climb the blocks to a
fun move through a small roof (15 metres) and then scramble up large blocks to the
anchors. (Be sure to have gear up to 4.") FFA: (ground-up onsight) Brandon Pullan,
Derrik Patola, August 2004.

First Buttress

Driving along the dirt road on the waterfront past the turnoff to the Rehab Centre, you
will quickly (100 metres) be in a clearing looking up at a rock buttress consisting of a
series of corners on good rock above a shale band. Park here. Walk south along the
road to the first little hill (50 metres) and start looking for a flagged trail. If you don't
find it, bushwhack toward the talus slope that leads up just left (south) of the cliffs.
"Stuck in a Jam" requires a rap in from the top. The rest of the routes are accessed by
hiking right, part way up the talus trail, to the base. If you hike north across the top

from "Stuck in a Jam" you will find
another set of bolts marking the top of
an off-width project that would be
about 50 metres of 5.10+ up a corner
with a birch tree at half height. Again,
routes are described from right to left,
that is, north to south.

10 Stuck In a Jam
23 Metres   5.9

 ★★

The is the northmost route, just to the
north of the ice route "April Showers."
Rappel in from the top of the bluff; find
the bolts near a clearing with pine trees.
Rappel (23 metres) to a good ledge (25
metres up from base) with two bolts.
This is a really good route, with very
good rests between difficult moves, and
a crack that eats up pro and offers
excellent jams. Follow the sustained
finger to fist crack. Gear to 3." FA: S.
Charlton, R. Treneer, Septembber 1996

11 Six-foot Roof
40 Metres   A2

 ★★

Here's a good intro to long aid routes.
This route is on the north-facing wall,
just left of the dirty chimney that in the
winter forms up as "Alexinova" (WI 3).
Avoid the shale band and start by beginning 3 metres right of crack line. Climb
the thin seam up left through roof and
traverse left to the main crack line.
Work up the crack and out the large
roof. Continue up the crack through a
slot, move right and climb easily to the
top. Belay from the tree. FA:
C. Chapman, R. Reed, August 1997.

12 Rehearsal   20 Metres 5.11+

 ★★★

An unrepeated line that deserves to be
a classic. This wild route made the
cover of an *Outcrops* newsletter. Climb

RANDY REED

Ryan Treener on Rehearsal, 5.11+.

the continuous finger-hand crack through the right-facing corner and roof. There is a bolt anchor at the top. FFA: R. Treneer, 1999.

13 Owens & Wong   15 Metres   5.8?

This is an easy crack route, but not very good. (No wonder it's named for a pair of famous porn stars). From the same start as "Teenage Porn Stars," move out left. FFA: Matt Pellet, Mark Powell.

14 Teenage Porn Stars   20 Metres   5.8   ★★

Start at the top of easy ledges to the right of the approach gully. Climb up the sizable dihedral past two roofs, using the undercling exit to the left. There is a rappel station at the top. Take gear to 3."   FA: R. Treneer, M. Pellet, 1997.

Alpine Outing Wall

This is a fine climbing area that still has a number of potential routes on cliffs to either side. Park at the Rehab Centre and walk south 75 metres to a dirt road that skirts south along the bottom of the cliffs. Or drive down this back road for 700 metres to a small breakwater point with a small rock beach. This is just past the fork in the road where a house driveway is on the right. Go left and park at this breakwater pullout. Hike 100 metres further down the road past a landing that has a camping trailer parked on it. You should find a cairn marking the trailhead; if not, just thrash into the bush for the wall. There is not a distinct path, but the wall comes into view as you climb a talus debris cone. Keep your eyes open; one hike into this wall in the 90's brought us within a step of a loaded leg hold trap.

Descent: The only good descent on Alpine Outing Wall is by rappelling down "Cedar Haven." The ice climb "Alpine Outing" (WI 4) forms in the wet, loose gully that splits the wall. The rap station is at the top of the gully. Rappel by the loose pinnacle down approximately 25 metres to a chain rappel station that is not visible from the top. The second rappel goes directly down over the top of a tall cedar tree. At this point you may see another cedar tree in a tight corner with old webbing around it indicating a rappel (13 metres). This tree can be used, but the stance is small and cramped.

15 Yonder   27 Metres   A2

Thrash up the the 30 metres of 4th class terrain through a shale band. Start right of the birch tree (fixed anchor). FA: S. Hamilton.

16 Sensuality   45 Metres   5.8

Start left of the birch tree and follow a splitter crack straight up to fixed anchors. FA: M. O'Brien, C. Jackson, September 1995.

17 Let's Be Frank (2 pitches)   72 Metres   5.8+   ★★★

This route was done after "Cedar Haven." Scott and Dave Nix cleaned it up before the Scotts returned to climb it. Scramble up a loose, stepped slope and start at the top of

RANDY REED

Alpine Outing Wall. Dirty Loose Bitch follows the crack at the far left, and Cedar Haven connects the line of three trees left of center.

an old fixed rope at the four-bolt anchor about 5 metres off the talus floor. Pitch 1: Climb up and left past a bolt onto a big ledge. An incredible crux involves a wicked mantle up onto the next ledge. Move right, and then up and around the corner (10 metres) to a gear belay (1/2" – 2"). Pitch 2: Work up the first obvious vertical crack (There is a possible gear belay about half way). Finish at a pair of top bolts. Rappel down "Cedar Haven." Take gear to 3", since there is only one bolt. FFA: Scott Morgan (pitch 1), S. Hamilton (pitch 2), 1994.

18 **Let's Be Frank, Direct Start** (1st pitch) 20 Metres C2

Even the first ascentionists listed this route as not worth climbing. It's likely too loose to go free. Climb right from the initial belay and up through the overhang. FA: Rene Lebel, R. Reed.

19 **Let's Be Frank Variation** (2nd pitch) 45 Metres 5.10? ★ ★

From the first gear belay stance, continue right 5 metres further on the ledge and belay in a dihedral with a fine crack.

Follow the vertical corner crack straight up through tougher laybacks to the top. There are bolts at the top anchor. Rappel down "Cedar Haven." Take a standard rack, as there is only one bolt. FA: S. Morgan (pitch 1), S. Hamilton (pitch 2), 1994.

*Alex Holowaty seconds
Let's Be Frank Variation.*

20 Cedar Haven
(2 pitches)   65 Metres   5.8+

 ★ ★

The start of this route is the
same as for "Let's Be Frank;"
scramble up a loose, stepped
slope, start at the top of an old
fixed rope with a four bolt
anchor (about 5 metres off the
talus floor) and work past a bolt
onto a big ledge to attack the
cruxy mantle. Then, head left
up past several more cedars to
the rappel/belay station and
work from there up the easiest
line to the top. There is a bolted
belay station that is hidden
from above and difficult to
locate while on rappel. (It is
almost a full 25 metre rappel to
get to the bolt station). This is the main rappel route out of this area. FA: Dave Nix,
Mike Holowaty, Tyler Bragnalo.

21 Double Bypass (2 pitches)   65 Metres   5.9   ★

This variation of "Cedar Haven" trends right on and around the corner once above the
first cedar tree squeeze. There are a variety of options above, some with interesting
runouts. FA: S. Charlton, Ryan Treneer, Shafton Thomas.

22 Dirty Loose Bitch (2 Pitches)   65 Metres   5.9

Just left of the gully, head up the fine clean crack. This route was generally considered
tough for its grade, but during a visit in 2002, it appeared that a significant block had
fallen off the top of the route. The finish may now be more difficult, or impossible.
Take a rack to go with the two bolts. FA: Scott Hamilton, Eric Abuluar.

Tundra Wall

While hunting for some of the lines that Shaun Parent had hinted about in the previous guide, a whole new wall was uncovered. About 100 metres right of "American
Demon," the area proved to have about a dozen dirty lines. A handful of them have
cleaned, and proven to be long, challenging routes.

The most useful landmark here is "Treeline Gully," which wanders up through the middle of the wall. The first three climbs listed are in the process of being developed on the upper curved wall to the right of "Treeline Gully." These routes have some bolts and have been climbed. The rest of the bolts and cleaning will probably have been done by the time this book is completed.

23 Aurora Borealis   40 Metres   5.11?

15 bolts. Using the large crack and some face holds, meander up to the arête and smear your way to the top. FA: B. Pullan.

24 Umiaks   45 Metres   5.10-5.12

15 bolts. This devious, blank-looking wall has lots of hidden features. FA: B. Pullan.

25 Wooly Mamooth Ain't So Wooly   45 Metres   5.11?

18 bolts. This route works up the curving wall to the crack near the top. FA: B. Pullan.

26 Treeline Gully   60 Metres   V   Scramble

Right of Inukshuk, follow the winding gully chocked with trees to the top. Clip the fixed pins and slung trees on the way. FA: B. Pullan, D. Patola, Fall 2004.

27 Inukshuk   60 Metres   5.10+    ★ ★ ★

While this route is great fun, it may still need a little cleaning. Pitch 1: Follow the crack right, then work up and left along the flake to get up and under roof. Pitch 2: Work up the corner roof crack to attain a face crack that goes to the top. Needs gear up to 4." FA: B. Pullan, D. Hereema, Fall 2004.

28 Musk Ox On Morphine   25 Metres   5.11b   ★ ★ ★

Approximately 12 bolts, on very clean granite. From under the large roof left of Inukshuk, delicately work up the slab, with some demanding moves, to a vertical face. This face leads to the anchors on the top of the first pitch of Inukshuk. FFA: B. Pullan, D. Hereema.

29 Polar Bear Express   50 Metres   5.11a   ★ ★

This is one fun, long, tough crack. Start uphill and right around the corner from Jenga. Ascend a series of ledges to get into the crack. The crux is near the middle. Needs gear up to 2." FA: B. Pullan, D. Hereema, Fall 2004.

30 Jenga (2 Pitches)   65 Metres   5.10b/c   ★ ★ ★

BOOM. There it is. A huge wall, made up of horizontal layers of hexagonal rails—what a crazy climb. It is long, exposed and sustained, with about 30 bolts) This route is of really odd rock, with big holds. Pitch 1: Follow bolts through windy sections up to the belay station. Pitch 2: Cruise the crux to the top. FA: B. Pullan; FFA: B. Pullan, D. Hereema, Jason Thorne.

Cam-a-Lot (5.10b) follows the long crack/chimney line just left of the prominent left face.

31 Off-width Crack(?)   35 Metres?   5.8?

Legend has it that, 50 metres right of "American Demon" is an off-width crack at the right end of a giant, square, clean roof. Look for slings in the crack. FA: S. Parent

Chiller Pillar Wall

This remote bastion offers spectacular views of the Sleeping Giant, Pie Island and (on a clear day) Isle Royale. The cliffs are similar in scale to Palisade Head in Minnesota, except that they are a few hundred metres from the water. The scenery, combined with the proximity to the lake, add a fantastic element of raw weather and extreme geography. Ironically, it is one of the least climbed areas in Thunder Bay. Drive down the dirt road just before the Rehab Centre. Continue past Alpine Outing Wall and go three kilometres until you get to a small clearing on the right. Park there and find the trail that leads quickly up onto the boulders. (It may still have some blue flagging tape).

Routes are listed from right to left.

32 American Demon (3 Pitches)   70 Metres   5.8, A2+   ★ ★ ★

Have an exciting adventure in aiding on this prominent face, with its well-cleaned crack on the upper section. Pitch 1, A2+: Climb a 5.8 crack to a ledge, and then aid up the thin crack. (This was a spectacular and intimidating section of the climb prior to '98; a now-fallen arrowhead-shaped flake below threatened to split you in half if you fell). The pitch ends at a bolted belay. Pitch 2, A2: Ascend an expanding right-facing corner and then traverse right to the beautiful hand crack. This leads to a rivet ladder that trends left at the top to a second belay. Pitch 3, 5.8: Top out by climbing a

Shaun Parent on the FA of American Demon.

short crack to the top. Descend by
rappelling the route. Take gear to
3" and rurps to baby angles.
FA: S. Parent, Scott Kress, 1981.

33 Tag (2 Pitches) 60 Metres 5.11a

 ★ ★ ★

Pitch 1: Beautiful jamming leads to a
cruxy finger lock and great gear all the
time (5.10b). Pitch 2: Adventurous
face climbing with nuts and good gear
leads to a hand crack in a roof (5.11a).
Rappel from rings. Old "Pokey"…?
FFA: D. Benton, J. Hammerich, 2001.

34 Cream & Suga 5.11a

 ★ ★ ★

"Fantastically varied, sporty trad
climb. All good gear whenever you need it." - Dave Benton. May be the old "Pokey"…?
FA: J. Hammerich, D. Benton, November, 2001

35 Pokey Kitty   40 Metres   A3

Climb the same block as for "Pokey Puppy." Then ascend the right of two facing
cracks. FA: J. Anfossi, S. Morgan, October, 1993.

36 Pokey Puppy   40 Metres   A2

At the right end of the cliffs, climb onto a large block. Then aid up the left crack to a
small roof, and a pair of bolts.   FA: S. Parent, S. Kress.

37 April Fools (2 Pitches)   40 Metres   A2

15-20 metres right of "Pokey Kitty," start up a small right-facing dihedral and crack for
about 25 metres to a ledge with a boulder belay. Then head out left for 5 metres and
up some smaller cracks to a ledge. On the first ascent, the lead tried going left (to a
fall) and then right (to another fall, which sent Julian to the hospital). Bolts may be
required above, on what is said to be a "nice looking" one or two pitches to the top.
FA: S. Morgan, J. Anfossi, April, 1994.

38 Test of Patience   25 Metres   A3   ★ ★ ★

Just right of "Stuffin' Martha's Muffin," and ending at that rappel anchor, thread a
tenuous route up a series of discontinuous cracks and seams. This route is pretty
gear-intensive; the suggested rack includes a double set of TCU's, cams to 2," many

blades, four rurps, and assorted beaks and bashies. FA: R. Reed, S. Charlton, 1997.

39 Stuffin' Martha's Muffin

25 Metres   5.10c (or C2)

Ascend the finger crack splitting a large white wall. It leads into a stretchy off-width-to-hand crack, before finally ending at a 2-bolt rappel station. The first ascent was done on aid, and rated at C2. Have gear to 3." FA: J. Anfossi, Cory Davis. FFA: Ryan Treneer, 1997.

40 Right Ski Track

15 Metres   5.10d

Beside "Placebo," ascend the right-hand crack to the same old blue (grey) sling.

41 Placebo

15 Metres   5.9

A few feet to the right of "Cam-A-Lot," climb the left crack to the old blue (grey) sling.

Stuffin Martha's Muffin (5.10c) is on the left. Test of Patience ends just below the small roof.

42 Cam-A-Lot (2 Pitches)   68 Metres   5.10b(5.9) ★ ★ ★

This route is the crag's classic off-width to finger crack. Brendan Waye first climbed it with the aid of one sling, and named it "Meteor Shower." Pitch 1: Begin climbing the left hand crack, stemming as needed. Then shift to the right hand crack. At about 20 metres, a green sling may still tell the history of Brendan Waye's first ascent. Stay to the left in the large chute, stemming up a hand crack to the bolted belay station (5.10b, 50 metres). Have extra cams, sizes one to 3! Pitch 2: This 18 metres of 5.8 choss is not recommended. It is not known whether there is an anchor at its top. FA: Brendan Waye; FFA: S. Morgan (pitch 1), J. C. Debeau (pitch 2), 1995.

43 1-900-HARDCOR   27 Metres   5.10b R

This line climbs the right-facing corner up to a group of loose roofs. Climb the open book, then move left on sketchy gear behind loose blocks. Continue up and then trend right past 2-3 pitons and finally reach a pair of pins with slings as a belay.

Mike Bragg and Leah Knutson on Spiral Galaxy.

The line above is more difficult, and is presumably virgin. There are three bolts on the route, but it needs three pins. FA: (aid) S. Parent, S. Kress, 1990. FFA: J. Anfossi, S. Morgan.

44 Right Hand Man
(2nd pitch)
22 Metres   5.10a

 ★ ★

This route was originally done as a second pitch variation of "Illusion Solution." From the bolt belay on that route, weave up some dubious flakes and onto a right hand-facing wall. Follow the fun hand crack to the top, where there are rappel anchors. Take clean gear to 3." FA: (TR solo) J. Anfossi, 1992.

45 Right Hand Man Direct (1st pitch)
40 Metres   5.10, A1

 ★ ★

A thin, mean crack splits the whitish wall, at a corner with two fixed pins. Work past the pins and up a face with three bolts. A relentless crack rises up to a cruxy traverse left. Saunter up to the belay ledge via the path of least resistance (a steep crack) to the 2-bolt belay on "Illusion Solution." From there, climb "Right Hand Man" to the rappel anchors. Take extra small nuts. FA: Ryan Treneer, Randy Reed, 1997.

46 Illusion Solution (2 Pitches)   65 Metres   5.9, A1

Pitch 1: Climb a pair of flakes to the small roofs. Then work right to some finger cracks (aid). Work up and further right to a standing belay with two bolts. Pitch 2: Head left up the flakes to the pine tree and then up the crack to the top. FA: S. Morgan (Pitch 1), J. Anfossi (Pitch 2), 1992.

NICK BUDA

Jen Haink on Saucisson, 5.10c.

47 **Spiral Galaxy** (2 Pitches)   32 Metres   5.7   ⟍ ★ ★ ★

Just right of "Beam Me Up Scotty," climb up an easy crack to the roof and traverse right onto a ledge to set up a belay. Climb up and left (crux) to anchors on "Beam Me Up..." Have some big gear, to 3.5." FA: S. Parent, Scott Kress, 1981.

48 **Saucisson**   5.10c   ★

Slashing straight up the blunt prow of the Peeping Squaw, a broken crack rises to a two metre roof. Traverse out and pull the lip (crux), wander up and slightly left on sustained (5.9) hand cracks. Have a multitude of 1"-3" pieces. FFA: D. Benton, M. Pellet, November, 2001.

49 **Beam Me Up Scotty**   32 Metres   5.10a   ★ ★ ★

Climb the dihedral/crack system (passing a piton) to the large ledge and then work right (1 bolt) up the face past three bolts to a fixed belay. There is a rap station for the descent. Gear needed includes one piton. FA: J. Anfossi, S. Morgan, September 1992.

50 **Beam Me Up Scotty variation**   32 Metres   5.11?

Climb the open book (passing a piton) crack up to the large ledge on "Beam Me Up Scotty" and then go further right (1 bolt) about two metres and then up the face. There is a rap station for the descent. FA: J. Anfossi, S. Morgan, Sept. 1992.

The next routes are around the corner, on the west face of Peeping Squaw Lookout.

51 **Rescue Route**   20 Metres   5.6

Head up the gully and then right onto the large buttress. FA: J. Anfossi, Walter Mann.

52 **Quasar** (2 Pitches?)   30 Metres?   5.8

Just to the right of "The Web," climb up to the tree and then head left past the tree. Go up a ramp to below the roof and traverse left beneath the roof, and try to find some gear that might reduce the risk of a dramatic pendulum here. Belay at the clump of birch trees. Climb up the blocky face that the Lookout is attached to, and top out at a large pine tree. There is a descent route to the left of the pine tree. FA: S. Parent, Mitz Bandiera, Chris Hrykynan, August 1991.

53 **The Web**   22 Metres   5.8   ★

Climb up the corner, using the left face, to the block on top. FA: Julian Anfossi, Shaun Bent.

"Space Walk," is located across a rock gully left of Peeping Squaw Lookout.

54 **Space Walk** (2 Pitches)   22 Metres   5.7+

Scramble up the rock gully left of the Peeping Squaw lookout. At the top of the gully is a shale band between two orange-colored headwalls. Pitch one (5.6): Climb up to the alcove, then go left and climb steep steps angling left and up. Half way up the steps, squeeze right between rock and bushes. Climb up to set a belay on the pie-shaped ledge. Pitch 2: Go straight up the open book crack on the right side of the division in the wall. It gets cruxy near top of this 10-metre section (5.7+). FA: Bill Konkol, Phil Lemieux, June, 1991.

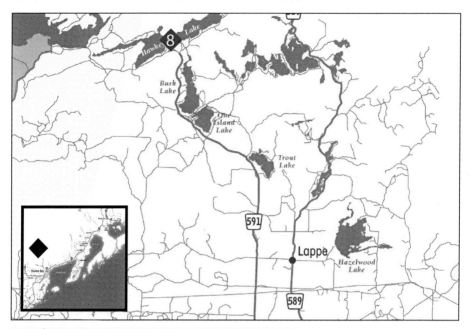

◆8 Hawkeye Lake

Route Character Sport – 0; Trad – 0, Mixed – 1, Toprope – 3, Multi-pitch – 1

Difficulty	
5.8–	1
5.9	1
5.10	0
5.11+	2

Travel   Drive time – 25 min., Hiking time – boat-only (or ice) access

Getting There: Go north on Red River Road/Hwy 102 from Hwy 11/17 out of
Thunder Bay. Turn right (northeast) onto Mapleward Road (10.4km). Follow this
road northeast for approximately 20 minutes (24.4km). Turn right at the fork in the
in the road; there is a brown sign that says "Hawkeye Lake." Continue 200m on
paved road, then turn left at the sign that says "Kay's Landing." Another 500m on a
dirt road leads to a public beach. The cliffs are on the north side of the lake, about
250m from the beach.

This cliff is situated on Crown land, on the far north side of Hawkeye Lake from a
public beach. Rob Dynes and various friends that frequented his bush camp identified and climbed these routes on a few weekends in the spring of 1996. All these
routes are face climbs, done on toprope. There is still significant potential here for difficult overhanging routes. There are presently no access issues. Use the public access
beach for parking and boat launching. In the winter, these routes are accesible over the
lake ice.

Looking up from a kayak at Cannibalistic Hamster, 5.9

ALEX JOSEPH

Camping

As this site is on Crown land, bush camping at the cliff is a likely option. Or, see Trout Lake Scout Camp, 30 km northwest of Thunder Bay via Hwy 102. They offer tenting & cabins. Call (807) 623-4446 for information

Swimming

Hawkeye Lake warms up by late May and can be warm into September.

1 **Protein Diet**

18 Metres   5.6

A real dirty face that needs a lichen exterminator. FA: Karen Stille, 1996.

2 **Mostly Harmless**

25 Metres   5.11+

A 5.8 face that quickly goes to vertical and then overhanging. FA: Rob Dynes, 1996.

3 **Bat In the Hole**   25 Metres   5.11+

A vertical to overhanging face route. FA: S. Bent, Don Salonen, 1996.

4 **Cannibalistic Hamster** (2 pitches) 55 metres   5.9

This route was bolted in Spring 1996, accessed by crossing the lake ice. Amazingly, no one was back to grab the FFA for nearly a decade. Pitch 1: (7 bolts, 27m) Begin at the left edge of the big slab/face and traverse right to the first bolt. Then follow the bolts through two small cruxes to the ledge and belay station. Alternate Pitch 2: Step right around the corner and work up 10m on thin pro, past at least one bolt without a hanger, to the rap station. Pitch 2: (4 bolts, 28m) Go straight up from the belay using cracks. Continue up the steep crack and flake to the left, past another bolt with no hanger and then up the easiest line, finding three more bolts above. There are belay stations with chains near the top. FA: (pitch 1) Rob Dynes, Dave Hrycyszyn, 1996; FFA: J. Childs, A. Joseph, August 2005.

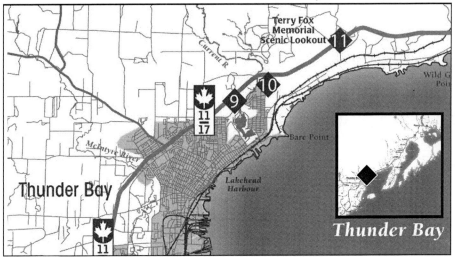

 ⑨ The Bluffs

Route Character Sport – 2, Trad – 41, Toprope – 76, Mixed – 0, Multi-pitch – 0

Difficulty
5.8–	86
5.9	10
5.10	18
5.11+	8

Getting There: The bluffs are located within Centennial Park on the northeast side of the city, north of Boulevard Lake.

From the east, exit off of the Trans Canada Highway (Highway 11/17) onto Hodder Ave. Go south on Hodder Avenue (also labeled Highway 11B/17B) about one km to Arundel Street. Turn right (west) onto Arundel Street and go less than one km. The Centennial Park lookout and parking lot is on the right, to the north of Boulevard Lake and Arundel St.).

From the west, exit off of the Trans Canada Highway to go right (south) on Balsam Street. Then make two immediate left turns onto Hudson Ave. about one km and Hudson St. turns into Arundel Street. Turn left (north) into the Centennial Park lookout and parking lot (north of Boulevard Lake and Arundel St.).

Park in the lot in Centennial Park overlooking the Sleeping Giant and head east down the path. Routes are listed from parking lot eastward, and from left to right as facing the cliff. Bouldering begins below the parking lot.

Some areas had been climbed and listed in the older guides for The Bluffs. These areas are the Willy Makit Wall located just past the parking lot, Betty Won't Bluff a couple minutes walk further along, and Sabre Wall which is a bouldering area just past Fancy Footing Wall.

This is a great place to get a lot of climbing/bouldering in, and it's the most likely place to find other climbers. With good views and a south orientation, it's a favoured spot for colder days.

Access Issues

These cliffs are located within an urban park – Centennial Park.

History

This area has been the focus of Thunder Bay's toproping for the last 25+ years. The Bluffs routes offers short traditional leading, as well as many face climbing opportunities. There are few uncontrived first ascents left here. Given the height, ease of top access and the very public venue, there are few sport routes at The Bluffs. Bolting for sport routes is frowned upon at this climbing area, although a number of routes have discreet top anchors.

One may find the grading difficult here. To the pioneers that established many of these routes, 5.8 must have been as hard as 5.12 seems today. To respect their efforts, some of the easier grades may feel harder then they are listed and this guide will respect that relic of Thunder Bay's early climbing history. Also, remember that route ratings are usually based on the overall difficulty of a climb. Shorter routes can often have very hard moves, compared to their overall rating. Where the sandbag factor is particularly severe, more recent consensus grades have been added to the route description.

Swimming

Cool off with a quick dip in the swimming area nearby in Boulevard Lake.

Routes are described in order from left to right.

Willy Makit Wall

1 That's All   8 Metres   5.5
On a west-facing wall, just right of a corner.

2 Giving Up   8 Metres   5.6
Beside "That's All" on the corner.

3 Oh Man   8 Metres   5.5

4 Ish   8 Metres   5.9

5 Give 'Er   8 Metres   5.10

6 Rad Rules   8 Metres   5.7

7 Try It, You'll Hate It   8 Metres   5.8

8 Third Try   8 Metres   5.6
In a southeast-facing corner.

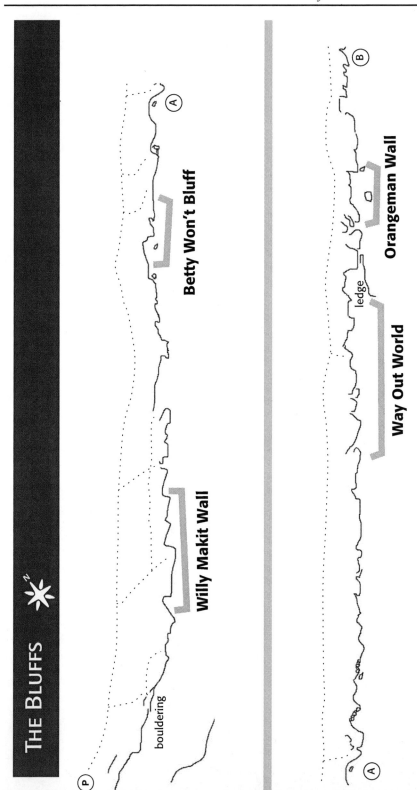

THE BLUFFS

Betty Won't Bluff

Willy Makit Wall

bouldering

Orangeman Wall

Way Out World

ledge

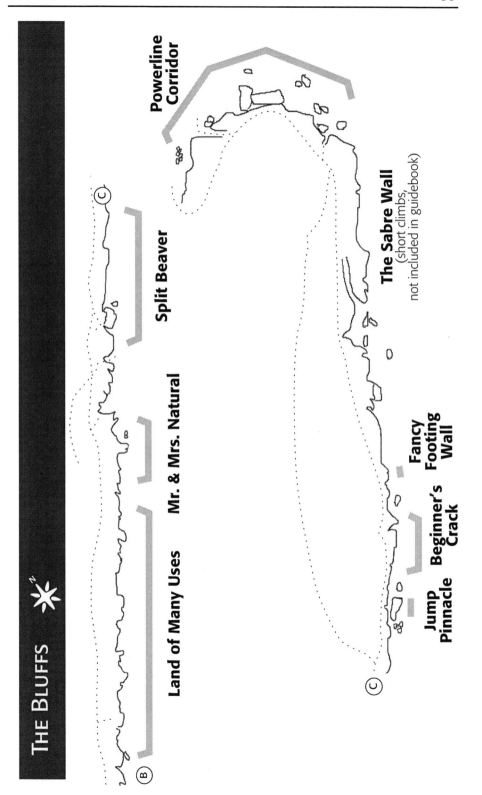

THE BLUFFS

N

Land of Many Uses

Mr. & Mrs. Natural

Split Beaver

Powerline Corridor

The Sabre Wall
(short climbs,
not included in guidebook)

Fancy Footing Wall

Beginner's Crack

Jump Pinnacle

B

C

C

THE BLUFFS

WAY OUT WALL

Wayout World Wall
21 Freak Street
22 Love Connection
23 Rum Doodle Bar & Grill
26 Up Yours

Orangeman Wall
27 Block Buster
28 Loose Rockfall
30 Exocet
31 Orange Crush
32 Passing Grade
33 Lemon Lime
34 Yellow Chimney
35 Rockwork Orange

36 Rockwork Orange Direct
37 Above and Beyond
38 Rockwork Orange Right
39 Nipple Mania
40 Alice In Wonderland
41 Joy Division

Land of Many Uses
44 The Walk
45 Ogre Face Left
46 Ogre Face Right
47 Gardener's Book
48 Garden's Edge
49 Gardening Slot
50 Trisuli Basaar
51 Unknown
52 Antagonist
53 Dance of the Ballerina
54 Just a Quicky
55 Poony's Pie
57 Root Cellar
58 Short and Sweet
59 Gardener's Tips
60 No Hang Ups
62 Mrs. Natural
63 Steroid King
64 Mr. Natural

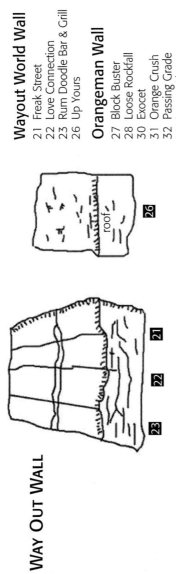

ORANGEMAN WALL

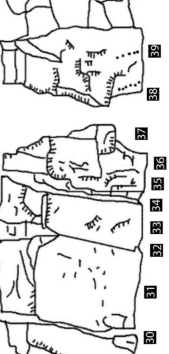

Split Beaver

66 Impossible Dream
67 Galaxian
68 Galaxian Direct
69 Split Beaver
70 Zugspit
71 Erect Nipplephobia
72 Seam of Dreams
73 Snow-covered Chunky Nuts
74 Conquering Armies
75 Dancer
76 Medley
77 The Complex
78 Oltenrec
79 Unknown
80 Don't Jump
81 Psychosexual

LAND OF MANY USES

SPLIT BEAVER

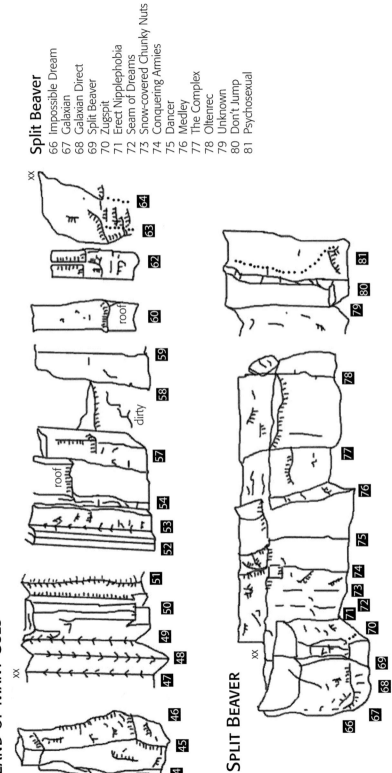

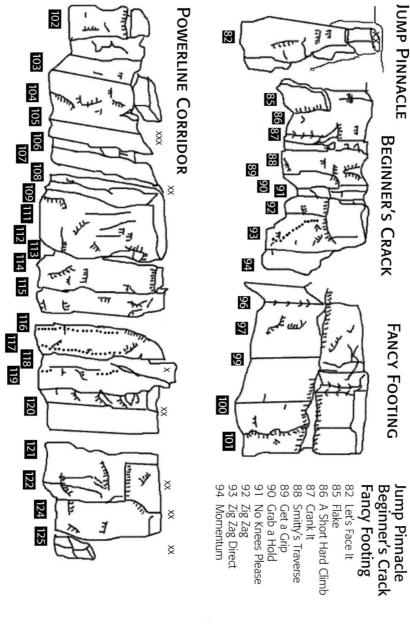

JUMP PINNACLE

BEGINNER'S CRACK

FANCY FOOTING

POWERLINE CORRIDOR

Jump Pinnacle
Beginner's Crack
Fancy Footing

82 Let's Face It
85 Flake
86 A Short Hard Climb
87 Crank It
88 Smitty's Traverse
89 Get a Grip
90 Grab a Hold
91 No Knees Please
92 Zig Zag
93 Zig Zag Direct
94 Momentum
96 Bibble
97 Chalk Sux
99 Loose Noose
100 Bestid Me/Randy's Crack
101 Fancy Footing

Powerline Corridor

102 Boulder Dash
103 Finger Lickin'
104 Flake 'til You Shake
105 Falling Rock
106 Twin Sisters
107 Corner Crack
108 Flying Dutchmen
109 Fudge Off
111 Hookenbladen
112 The Sick and the Afflicted
113 John and Ponchareli
114 Walk Up
115 Assgripper
116 Misconception
117 See Forest Flail
118 Richard's Crack
119 I'll Do This One
120 "C" is for Clowns
121 Partner
122 Guy's Dream
124 Coots
125 Shorty

9 **Second Try** 8 Metres 5.7

This route is in the next southeast-facing corner to the right of "Third Try."

10 **Edge of the Wave** 8 Metres 5.6

Climb the arête on the wave between the "First Try" and "Second Try."

11 **First Try** 8 Metres 5.5

In yet another another southeast-facing corner, with some spruce trees above.

Betty Won't Bluff

Again, routes are described in order from left to right.

12 **I've Had It** 8 Metres 5.5

This route is on a south-facing wall. A flake and a block on the ground are just to its right, and a cedar tree is to the south.

13 **Give Up** 8 Metres 5.4

This route is on a southwest-facing wall, just to the right of a corner.

14 **Cannonball Run** 8 Metres 5.8

A quick little face route.

15 **I Enjoy 69** 8 Metres 5.5

This route follows a classic fist crack on the southwest corner.

16 **Farewell Friends** 8 Metres 5.6

This is a nicely-sized hand crack.

17 **Cheapscape** 8 Metres 5.4

In the corner—dig in with that shoulder!

18 **Hine-a-kin** 8 Metres 5.5

Another straightforward hand crack on the south side, right of the corner that holds "Cheapscape."

19 **Snorter** 8 Metres 5.8

A clear, but not simple, finger crack.

20 **Yabob** 8 Metres 5.7

Work the finger crack to a layback at the top.

Wayout World Wall

21 Freak Street 8 Metres 5.6

Just left of a right-facing edge and right of the chossy corner, this left-trending finger crack is a little tricky in the beginning.

22 Love Connection 8 Metres 5.7

The middle finger crack, with spruce trees in front, has a bouldery start. There are two bolts at top.

23 Rum Doodle Bar & Grill 8 Metres 5.6

This route, which takes good gear, follows the left crack.

24 The Double O 8 Metres 5.7

A short face climb leads to stacked overhangs above. FA: Ken Smith, B. Konkol, 1990.

25 Booking Up 8 Metres 5.6

This line is on a southeast-facing wall below a park lookout. Climb left of the corner and right of the arête.

26 Up Yours 6 Metres 5.8

This route, 30 metres to the right of "Freak Street," tackles the south-facing wall with a nice roof about a third of the way up.

Orangeman Wall

Again, routes are described in order from left to right. There is a trail to the top 10 metres to the left of "Blockbuster."

27 Block Buster 6 Metres 5.7

Climb the large block at the bottom, then struggle up the flaring crack.

28 Loose Rockfall 6 Metres 5.6

Just to the right of "Block Buster," climb up the face and crack.

29 Sidewinder 8 Metres 5.8

Left of "Exocet."

30 Exocet 9 Metres 5.5 ★

Climb the nice finger/hands crack in the left corner (using the blank faces on either side) to the blocky ledge, then traverse right to the top. There is a two-bolt belay at the top.

31 Orange Crush 9 Metres 5.11b ★★

This route was called "Orangeman Wall" (5.7?) before it was freed. Either start to the right of "Exocet" or in the middle, decipher the thin face on smear footholds, and then negotiate the arête on the right to a high step finish.

32 Passing Grade

9 Metres   5.11a

This is the first aid route done at the Bluffs, and
before it was freed, was called "Tester Crack (A1)."
On the small seam to the right and behind the
arête used in "Orange Crush," climb the thin corner. Face holds on the right are the key. FFA:
Shawn Robinson, June 2004.

33 Lemon Lime

7 Metres   5.7

Climb the face to the right of "Passing Grade," and
either use the arête on your left or the crack in
"Yellow Chimney" on the right.

34 Yellow Chimney

6 Metres   5.5

Chris Joseph on Orange Crush, 5.11b.

Use whatever you like in the corner right of "Lemon Lime."

35 Rockwork Orange   8 Metres   5.6

Climb straight up right of the "Yellow Chimney" corner, using slanting cracks and
seams on the west side, left of the overhang. Then overcome the horizontal blocks
near the top.

36 Rockwork Orange Direct   8 Metres   5.8+    ★★★

Starting just under the overhang two metres off the ground on the right side, climb up to
the left and out on to the face, then up to the top. Along with gear to 2," takes one pin.

37 Above and Beyond   9 Metres   5.10d

Negotiate the roof (on "Rockwork Orange") head on, then climb up the corner to the
right. Don't go too far to the right, or you'll likely be slipping off onto the easier
"Rockwork Orange Right."

38 Rockwork Orange Right   9 Metres   5.7

Starting around the corner from the overhang, climb up, then traverse out left onto the
corner above the overhang.

39 Nipple Mania   9 Metres   5.8   ★

Right of "Rockwork Orange Right," climb straight up and over the lip to the slab.

Nick Buda on Gardener's Tips, 5.9

40 Alice In Wonderland   8 Metres   5.8–

10 metres right of "Nipple Mania," climb up the crack to a ledge on the left, then follow the arête to the top.

41 Joy Division   8 Metres   5.9

Start on the right side of the face to the right of "Alice In Wonderland." Climb up and traverse left, then up to a slopy finish, staying right of the corner to a small overhang at the top.

42 Keystone   8 Metres   5.10a

Being the Scenic Bluffs, this route 25 metres right of "Rockwork Orange." may have been climbed before Shawn and Nick tagged it. It's the hand crack with a chockstone half way up. FFA: Shawn Robinson, Nick Buda, Summer 2003.

Land of Many Uses and Mr. & Mrs. Natural Habitat Area

43 Crack Gringo   8 Metres   5.4

44 The Walk   8 Metres   5.7

Start on the left side of "Ogre Face." Traverse out onto that route, and climb straight up.

45 Ogre Face Left   8 Metres   5.9   ★

Start slightly off center left and negotiate the boulder move at the start (5.10a) and then up the slab to the top.

46 Ogre Face Right   8 Metres   5.10a

Do the right arête start (5.10d) and then traverse onto the slab and to the top.

47 Gardener's Book   9 Metres   5.8   ★

This route is a metre to right of the "Open Book." Work the solid layback moves in the middle. There is a two-bolt belay at the top. FA/FFA: M. Suchma, 1997.

48 Garden's Edge   9 Metres   5.10d

Climb the right arête beside the open book. There are two bolts at top.

49 Gardening Slot   9 Metres   5.10+   ★

Beside "Garden's Edge" and right around the corner, climb the hand/fist crack up to the overhanging off-width. FA/FFA: M. Suchma, 1997.

50 Trisuli Basaar   9 Metres   A2

Two metres right of "Gardening Slot," aid the small roof off the ground and finish left on the rivet ladder, or move right placing copperheads and rurps.

51 Unknown   9 Metres   5.8

Climb the corner using face holds and the thin crack.

52 Antagonist   9 Metres   5.6   ★

Climb the cracks running up the prow that juts out from the main cliff.

53 Dance of the Ballerina   6 Metres   5.8

A metre to the right of "Antagonist," climb up the slab with the corner on your left, to a tricky crux just below the top.

54 Just a Quicky   6 Metres   5.5

This climb goes up the chimney that has a roof right of the route near the top.

55 Poony's Pie   8 Metres   A1

Originally done as an aid route.

56 Mr. Put   8 Metres   5.5

57 Root Cellar   6 Metres   5.5

Start on either side of the slab and climb straight up past a small overhang on the right side.

58 Short and Sweet   6 Metres   5.7

Climb up the corner just to the right of the spruce tree on the ledge.

Steroid King, 5.9, follows the chalked handholds on the right.

59 Gardener's Tips

8 Metres   5.9   ★

Two metres to the right of "Short and Sweet," climb the fine finger crack running straight up the face.

60 No Hang Ups

8 Metres   5.9

First negotiate the roof, then work up the slab to the top.

61 Face This Nation   8 Metres   5.2

62 Mrs. Natural   6 Metres   5.5   ★

Climb up to the big crack splitting the large block at the top. There is a two-bolt belay at the top.

63 Steroid King   6 Metres   5.9   ★

This route is on the same block as "Mrs. Natural," but around the corner to the right. Power your way up the overhanging face. F.A.: Alex Joseph.

64 Mr. Natural   6 Metres   5.8+   ★

Right next to "Steroid King," climb the finger crack using a couple of face holds. There is a two-bolt belay at the top.

Split Beaver

65 Edward   8 Metres   5.4

66 Impossible Dream   8 Metres   5.6   ★

On the left corner of the block, negotiate the steep wall and hard slab finish.

Galaxian (L) and Split Beaver.

67 **Galaxian**   9 Metres   5.10b   ★★★

This enduring classic has also been soloed. Start left or right of the face without ignoring the central hidden foothold. Undercling through the crux, and you're up the crack to the top anchors and done. This route was retro-bolted for a while, ruining the history of the climb. The bolts have since been removed. FA: S. Parent, P. Dedi, 1981.

68 **Galaxian Direct**   9 Metres   5.11a   ★

Take it straight up the middle.

69 **Split Beaver**   10 Metres   5.5   ★★

Climb the larger crack to the right of "Galaxian." Gear to 4".

70 **Zugspit**   7 Metres   5.5   ★

Climb the right corner of the big block.

71 **Erect Nipplephobia**   6 Metres   5.10a

Climb the face next to "Zugspit," on small and crimpy holds.

72 **Seam of Dreams**   9 Metres   5.12

Climb the thin seam up the blank-looking wall. This route has been led, but not often! FA: S. Bent.

Conquering Armies, 5.7.

ALEX JOSEPH

73 Snow-covered Chunky Nuts

9 Metres   A3

A metre right of "Seam of Dreams," aid up the next-to-nothing-looking seam. FA: S. Hamilton, 1995?

74 Conquering Armies

9 Metres   5.7

 ★ ★

Climb the enticing, wicked crack. The cruxy second move is just high enough for Elvis to make an appearance. Gear to 3". FA: S. Parent, J. Murphy, 1981.

75 Dancer   9 Metres   5.7   ★

Climb the crack to the blocky finish.

76 Medley   7 Metres   5.5

Climb the arête to the ledge, and finish on "Dancer."

77 The Complex   9 Metres   5.8   ★

Climb the corner crack onto a ledge. Muscle up the overhanging wall to finish.

78 Oltenrec *(see photo color section)*   9 Metres   5.8

Climb the hand and fist crack up to the ledge, then dance up the slab to finish.

79 Unknown   7 Metres   5.10+

Start on the ledge. Climb the corner and then work yourself over to the slab on the right.

80 Don't Jump   10 Metres   5.6   ★ ★

Climb the left side of the large flake, using crack and face holds.

Jump Pinnacle.

81 **Psychosexual**   7 Metres   5.11a   ★

Starting in the middle of the face, climb halfway up, then work your way to the left and up to the top.

Jump Pinnacle,
Beginner's Crack and Fancy Footing Walls

82 **Let's Face It**   7 Metres   5.9   ★

Climb the north corner of the pinnacle, from a bouldery start. Top bolts on the pillar have replaced the previous awkward gear setup.

83 **Let's Face It Direct**   7 Metres   5.10c   ★★

This variation begins on the right. Climb a balancy crimper start to unseen holds above.

84 For Your Eyes Only 8 Metres 5.5

85 Flake 6 Metres 5.4

Climb up either side of the flake and then onto the bomber holds above.

86 A Short Hard Climb 6 Metres 5.10a

Start on the blank face using small crimpers. Work up using the sloping ledge to the right, then find the right side pull to finish. Sustained.

87 Crank It 6 Metres 5.8 ★

Just to the right of "A Short Hard Climb," climb up the parallel cracks.

88 Smitty's Traverse 6 Metres 5.6

Climb up the left arête and finish on the right.

89 Get a Grip 6 Metres 5.5

Climb up the crack to the right of "Smitty's Traverse."

90 Grab a Hold 6 Metres 5.5

Climb inside the chimney, and then up to the left.

91 No Knees Please 7 Metres 5.5 ★

Climb up the left arête and exit to the right.

92 Zig Zag *(see photo color section)* 7 Metres 5.7 ★ ★ ★

Follow the large crack up the middle, and then move to the right. To lead, have gear to 4."

93 Zig Zag Direct 7 Metres 5.10b ★ ★

This route might be what was formerly named "Shudder and Shake (5.9)." Start on the lower right face-arête and climb the face up and left.

94 Momentum 9 Metres 5.9

Start as for "Zig Zag Direct," but stay on the right side, using face holds and the crack.

95 Heidi's Horror 8 Metres 5.8

96 Bibble 6 Metres 5.7

Climb up the open book to the ledge. A harder version starts with stemming moves and then pulls up onto the face above the ledge (5.10b).

97 Chalk Sux 9 Metres 5.8-

This must be a Parent route. Climb up the face using side pulls and small ledges. Traverse right at the large ledge and work up the slab to the top.

98 Upper Dihedral 8 Metres 5.2

*Flake 'til You Shake (5.8) climbs
the face just left of the offwidth,
Falling Rock (5.7).*

99 Loose Noose
9 Metres   5.6

 ★

Climb the crack up to a
ledge. Then work up the
dihedral to the top.

100 Bestid Me/
Randy's Crack
9 Metres   5.9+

 ★

Climb the thin crack to a
ledge. Then tackle the overhanging fist crack!

101 Fancy Footing   4 Metres   5.5   ♀

Climb face holds up to the ledge just to the right of "Randy's Crack."

*Following the trail up and west from the Powerline Corridor, you may spot a short wall
east of the trail. The short routes on the Sabre Wall have been practice and bouldering
territory for many years, but no history of routes, names, etc. is available.*

Powerline Corridor

102 Boulder Dash   6 Metres   5.7   ♀
Climb the face around the the trail to the bluff top.

103 Finger Lickin'   6 Metres   5.9   ♀
Start on the block. Climb up the corner on small crimpy holds.

104 Flake 'til You Shake   7 Metres   5.8   ♀ ★ ★ ★
Work up small ledges and flakes to a long reach at the finish.

ALEX JOSEPH

*Andy Van Schaik on
Twin Sisters, 5.5*

SHAUN PARENT

105 Falling Rock

7 Metres   5.7

Climb the off-width crack
straight up to the top.

106 Twin Sisters

8 Metres   5.5   ★

Two cracks with huge blocks between them lead up to a tree at the top. This is a popular beginner's route—there's a two-bolt belay at the top.

107 Corner Crack   9 Metres   5.5   ★

Climb the crack in the corner until reaching the ledge, then do some wicked stemming between the two walls. There is a two-bolt belay anchor at the top. For leading, have gear to 3."

108 Flying Dutchmen   9 Metres   5.12a   ★★★

One of only two routes in the region contributed by climbers from overseas (Netherlands), this line has incredible beginning cruxes. Climb the overhanging corner all the way, following three bolts. Use anything that allows you to beat gravity, including underclings, smears and matches. The crux is a thin left crimp to a right hand pinch hold, all while your feet are madly trying to find some friction. The route gets easier above (5.10+). There is a bolted top anchor. FA: Martin & Ernesto, 1992.

109 Fudge Off   10 Metres   5.10+   ★

Goes up the overhanging off-width crack. FA: R. Treneer?

110 Project   10 Metres   A5

Start on the left-facing flake, and aid up the thin cracks. Have lots gear appropriate to thin cracks; rurps, peckers, knive blades, and big balls!

111 Hookenbladen   10 Metres   A3

Thin hooks and blades will get you up the small left-leaning crack. Aid up the blank face to the old bolt hole, then work into the thin seam that tends left. Frightening for the first 6 metres. FA: S. Hamilton, 1995?

112 The Sick and the Afflicted   10 Metres   5.12b   ★

Start below the flaring crack. Halfway way up, work your way onto the ledge and start up the crack (crux) and finally get to better holds. FA: J. C. Dubeau (A3); S. Bent (toprope), 1995.

113 John and Ponchareli   10 Metres   A2

Work up the thin crack on the left arête of "Walk Up." FA: S. Hamilton, 1995?

114 Walk Up   10 Metres   5.5   ★

Climb up the chimney and then onto the left corner.

115 Assgripper   9 Metres   5.8+   ★

Follow the fist to off-width crack in the middle of the face. Leaders need gear to 4". FA: S. Parent, P. Dedi, 1979.

116 Misconception   9 Metres   5.10d

Climb the right corner right of "Assgripper," and then work out onto the right face and on to the top.

117 See Forest Flail   9 Metres   5.10c    ★★

Restrict yourself to the face and the outside corner on the right. Balance is the key—Move delicately up the face, hanging off the right arête and stepping on it periodically. FA: Forest Latimer?

118 Richard's Crack   10 Metres   5.7   ★★

Climb in the corner, either laybacking the crack or using some of the face holds. There are anchors at the top, but leaders need gear to 6." FA: B. Konkol?

119 I'll Do This One   10 Metres   5.10c   ★★

Follow the thin seams right of "Richard's Crack." There's a weird finger move two-thirds of the way up. You might be cursing on this one, especially since some of the original holds have come off! There is a bolted belay anchor. FA: S. Parent, P. Mahoney (aid, 5.9, A2), 1983.

Assgripper, 5.8+.

ALEX JOSEPH

120 **"C" is for Clowns**   9 Metres   5.7   ★
Climb up the large crack, using the slopy ledges and the right side of the crack. There are two bolts at top.

121 **Partner**   7 Metres   5.5
Ten metres right of "C is for Clowns," climb the left side of a northwest-facing wall up to a ledge and then up a small face. There are two bolts at top.

122 **Guy's Dream**   7 Metres   5.8   ★
Start below the thin crack, and climb up (using some of the face holds) to a ledge. Work up the small roof to finish. There are two bolts at top. FA: G. Lauziere?

ALEX JOSEPH

See Forest Flail, 5.10c, is on the face just left of Richard's Crack, 5.7.

123 **Twenty Bucks**   7 Metres   5.8

Climb the face between "Guy's Dream" and "Coots "and then move left onto the upper face between "Guy's Dream" and "Partner." FA: B. Konkol, Frank Pianka, 1990.

124 **Coots**   7 Metres   5.6

Just next to "Guy's Dream," climb the crack up to the ledge on that route, and then traverse to the right onto the slab.

125 **Shorty**   7 Metres   5.4

Climb a crack up to the tree, then work through the blocky top. There are two bolts at top.

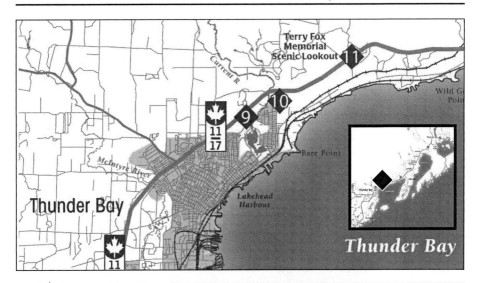

10 Water Tower

Route Character Sport 3; Trad 2; Toprope – 5, Mixed – 0, Multi-pitch – 0

Difficulty		
5.8–	7
5.9	1
5.10	2
5.11+	0

Getting There: Water Tower is in Current River, an area of Thunder Bay near the Current River. It is located on the east side of Hodder Ave. just south of Highway 11/17. Use the short, steep hill with the water tower on top as your landmark.

From Thunder Bay, drive east out Hodder Avenue until just before the Highway 11/17 junction. Turn right (southeast) onto a gravel road going up a hill to a tower. The cliffs are just to the south of the fenced-in tower.

This obscure area is is a lot like "The Bluffs," except that it's small, dirty, and tucked away in the bush. Most of the routes are face climbs. A number of them are sport routes, most protected by old (1990–91) bolts. The new routes, done in 2004, have equally new bolts. While the area is essentially fully developed, it is rarely climbed.

Access Issues

These cliffs are located on or near a private radio/tv tower station.

History

The Water Tower Wall is a little-known cliff on the east side of town near the Current River that has similar characteristics of "The Bluffs" in Thunder Bay. The developers who slyly put up these routes over two summers (1990–91) requested in an early 1990's "Outcrops" newsletter that any new routes should follow the automobile nomenclature.

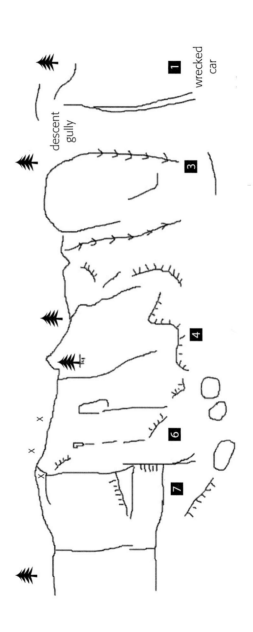

1 **Flat-bed Ford**   8 Metres   5.3

Just a short, easy slab route.

2 **Pop da Hood**   9 Metres   5.10b

Just left of "Camaro," travel up through balancy moves through a technical crux up to the top. Follows three bolts, and has top anchors. The route gets slabby near the anchor. FA: B. Pullan, N. Gingrich, 2004; FFA: B. Pullan, N. Gingrich, 2004.

3 **Camaro**   8 Metres   5.7

Love those curves! This climb is on a roundish buttress.

4 **VW Bus** 8 Metres   5.6

This is a great beginner climb, fun and easy, and set up with three bolts. Take a big reach across the center and up to the ledge, then cruise to the top anchors on good holds. Climb to the pine tree on the upper ledge.

5 **VW Bus with a Porsche Engine**   8 Metres   5.7

Find some hidden power; climb the finger crack left of "VW Bus."

6 **Dodge Challenger**   8 Metres   5.7+

There are three bolts at top of this route.

7 **Hemi Charger**   8 Metres   5.8+

Put the pedal to the metal when you tackle this roof problem.

8 **New Hemi Charger**   8 Metres   5.10b

Climb to the huge roof, haul up to the jug on the face, and clip. Use the arête and high step to a side pull. It's just a big boulder problem! The route has two bolts and a great anchor, off the tree at the top. FFA: N. Gingrich, 2004.

9 **Mom's Harley**   8 Metres   5.7

Work up the broken corner/crack system to the top. Just right of of the massive roof on "Hemi Charger," this route is easy to find. Have gear to 3". FFA: B. Pullan, 2004.

10 **4Runner**   8 Metres   5.9

Up the face crack that angles right. FFA: B. Pullan, N. Gingrich, 2004.

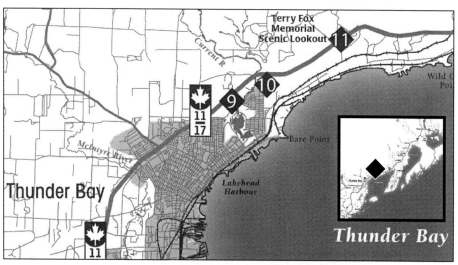

Thunder Bay

11 ▶ Terry Fox

Route Character Sport – 0, Trad – 1, Toprope – 6, Mixed – 0, Multi-pitch – 0

Difficulty		
	5.8–	1
	5.9	1
	5.10	3
	5.11+	2

Getting There: Go east out of Thunder Bay. 500 metres past Hodder Avenue, the cliffs are around the monument on the north side of the highway. Park in the convenient lot just at the base of the wall.

The small area just north of Thunder Bay that was cleared (and dynamited) to make room for the Terry Fox Memorial is surrounded by small and and very visible cliffs. It has some great views, but is rarely (and only discretely) climbed.

History

Numerous boulder problems and small climbs exist now on the cliffs below the monument on Highway 11/17, and unknown boulderers have probably done many more problems that are unrecorded. Dallas Markall and friends climbed a number of these routes prior to 1995, soon after the monument was constructed. A few are listed that were done below the monument on the east as well as in the recently-dynamited area east of the approach road.

Access Issues

These cliffs are located at a visitor's rest stop and monument. Keep a low profile. Bolting is not a good idea on the rock surrounding the monument.

Monument Area

1 Tweetie's Place   6 Metres   5.8
Climb the nice hand crack.

2 Dyno-mite   6 Metres   5.10a
Begin in the two-finger-pocket layback, and then throw a right-hand dyno to the
ledge. Work to the left from there. This is a one-move climb, but it's a great move!

3 By the Nails Arête   6 Metres   5.10c
Underclings lead to some nice edging and a few side-pulls. This dicey little line is
harder than it looks.

4 Unknown   8 Metres   5.11a

5 Jam the Scrub Brush   7 Metres   5.?
This nice short crack is easy to find; look for the steel brush jammed within...

Dynamited In Fall '95 Area

6 Unknown   8 Metres   5.10+
A lovely (though dusty) dynamited arête with a few dynamite holes left over.

7 I Saw Me an Ice Climber Today   8 Metres   5.11
First attempted in late November, 1995, on a sunny −15°C. day. The slabby, dusty
beginning leads to a smooth dihedral finish.

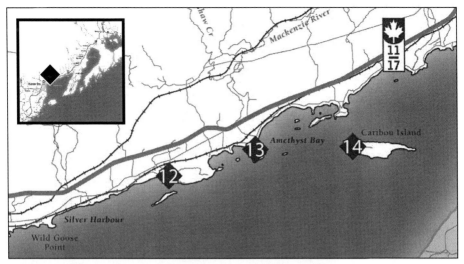

 **Silver Harbour**

Route Character Sport – 26, Trad – 35, Mixed – 5, Toprope – 28, Multi-pitch – 0

Difficulty		
5.8 –	40	
5.9	13	
5.10	26	
5.11 +	12	

Getting There: While you could park closer than the present 5- to 10-minute approach to the routes, it's best to keep a low profile with the local homeowners and the Conservation Authority. Park down in the Conservation Area lot (There might be a $2 parking fee). The path is about 150 metres back up the road and on the east side.

This is a great crag to lead on sport, trad or mixed routes, with steep challenging climbs and a sizable number of sport routes. With solid rock and easy setups, Silver Harbour is a popular area that has been more or less fully developed.

Access Issues

Silver Harbour Conservation Area is located about 15 minutes east of Thunder Bay off of Lakeshore Drive. The cliffs are located just north of the conservation area and are surrounded by cottages and a driveway on two sides. The Lakehead Region Conservation Authority does not allow climbing on their land. Do not camp in the conservation area.

Further down the "trail" to the east is the "Fifteen Minutes to Heaven" area developed in April, 1996. Climbs east of "Black Stallion Arête" are on privately-owned land and climbing is allowed by permission at present. That area is likely to stay available for climbing, as long as climbers keep a low profile, don't create traffic and parking problems, and avoid any damage to flora and fauna. Recent info has come to light from a

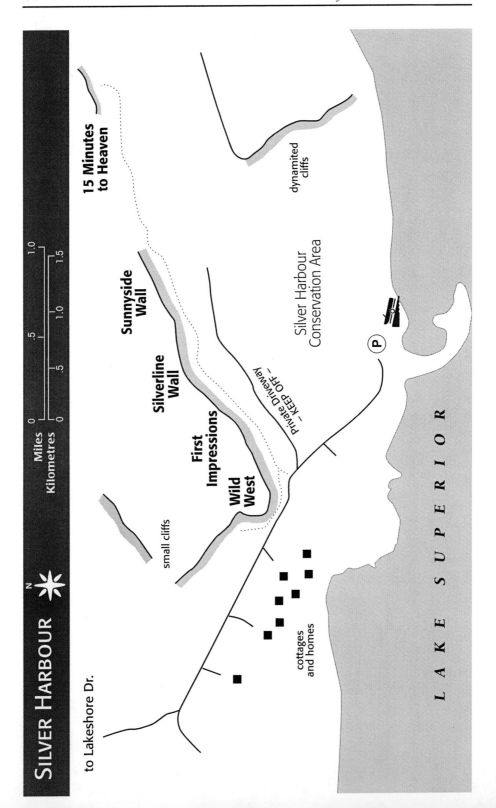

SILVER HARBOUR

N

Miles
Kilometres

0   .5   1.0
0   .5   1.0   1.5

to Lakeshore Dr.

15 Minutes
to Heaven

Sunnyside
Wall

Silverline
Wall

First
Impressions

Wild
West

small cliffs

Private Driveway
– KEEP OFF –

cottages
and homes

P

Silver Harbour
Conservation Area

dynamited
cliffs

LAKE SUPERIOR

SILVER HARBOUR

WILD WEST WALL

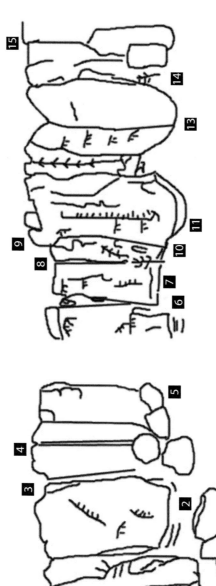

FIRST IMPRESSIONS

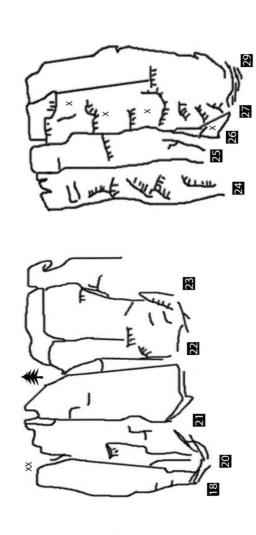

SILVER HARBOUR

SILVERLINE WALL

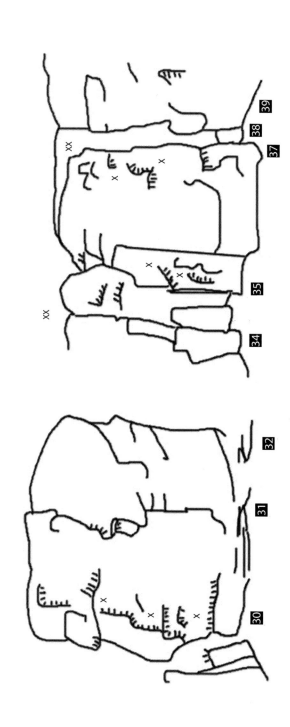

SILVER HARBOUR

SILVERLINE WALL

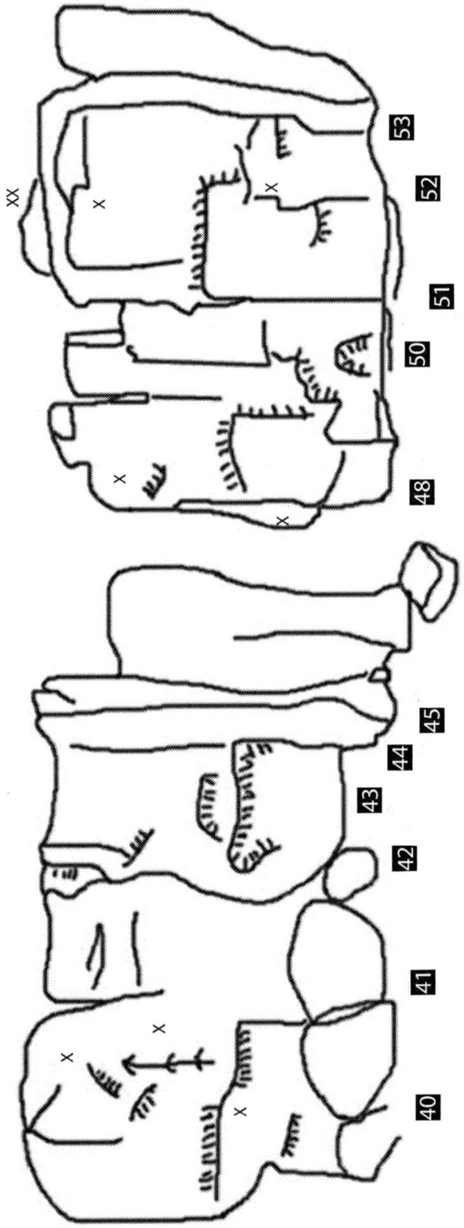

SILVER HARBOUR

SUNNYSIDE WALL

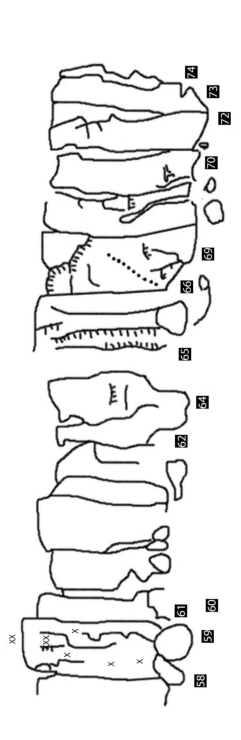

ORGASMATRON WALL

SILVER HARBOUR

15 MINUTES TO HEAVEN

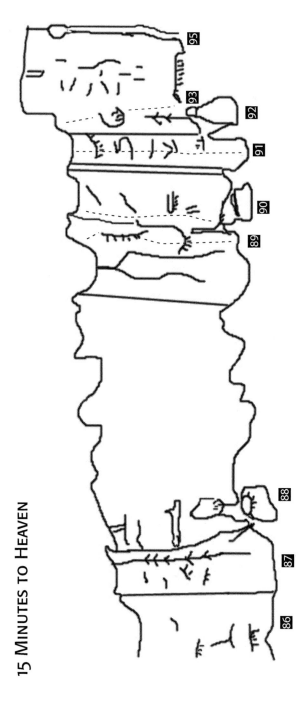

talk with an original member, about rare fauna on cliffs as well of falcon nesting sites. Keep the area clean and do as little habitat damage as possible.

History

Julian Anfossi and some friends took the lead in developing this area, as part of Julian's Lakehead University Outdoor Recreation project. They climbed a number of great routes, and left a legacy of incomplete projects. Many of the projects have since been ascended and a couple of new lines have been completed.

Swimming

There is a swimming area at the parking area/boat launch.

Fight Like a Brave, 5.8

Wild West Wall

Routes listed from left (west) to right (east).

1 Fight Like a Brave   9 Metres   5.8   ★

Climb left and up onto the face.

2 Righteous and the Wicked   6 Metres   5.9+

Start up the easy beginning to the dicey crux moves on the right-leaning crack.

3 Ferngully   8 Metres   5.5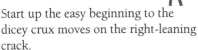

Climb up the obvious but overgrown crack.

4 Dedi Did It   8 Metres   5.8

 ★

This climb follows the lovely finger crack. The point of aid on Paul Dedi's first ascent (A1) has since been eliminated.   FA: P. Dedi, S. Parent, 1982.

Randy Reed on Dedi Did It, 5.8.

5 Every Which Way But Loose

9 Metres   5.8

Work straight up the solid fist crack.

6 Smok'n Gun 5.7

Climb the face on the right using ledges to the top.

7 Stretch To the Moon

9 Metres 5.11d

Climb the face route beside "Smok'n Gun" using the flakes and the thin seam. The route has two bolts, but take gear to 2" as well. FA: S. Hamilton.

8 Tan Lines 5.7

Use laybacks and jams to work up to the flake.

9 French Line

5.10c

Climb the slightly overhanging wall next to "Tan Lines" and up the balancy slab.

10 Don't Mess With Texas

5.6

Follow the crack using the ledges on the left.

11 Ever To Be Free

9 Metres   5.12a

Enjoy the overhanging laybacks in the thin hand crack. They lead to very steep, dicey rotten seams and edges to the top. Or aid (A2, when this route was known as "Never To Be Free") on gear including pitons and hooks.

Stretch to the Moon, 5.11d (above) and French Line(5.10c).

12 Wit of a Ninja

9 Metres 5.12a (?)   ★ ★

This long-running project at Silver Harbor finally went, but the grade is tentative. Climb a series of flakes, following four bolts up to the last move, which uses a small crimp to get a foot up and throw for the jug. FFA: B. Pullan, June 2004.

13 Orange Crush

5.9

Use a series of small ledges to climb the thin crack. Then work up to the harder moves near the top.

14 Electric Beach

5.9+

After pulling through the fist jams, be ready for the tough exit moves.

Dont Mess with Texas, 5.6

15 Happy Go Lucky   5.6

Ascend the crack to the horizontal, and then move onto the face to the right. Smile!

16 Be Happy and Get Lucky

10 Metres   5.10

Right of "Happy Go Lucky" and around the corner and downhill slightly, climb up the steepening face, traversing slowly left towards "Happy Go Lucky." Rejoin that route on the upper ledge and face. FA: A. Joseph, J. Childs, August 2005.

Wit of a Ninja, 5.12a(?).

17 Project

10 Metres 5.12?

An open project, this cleaned area follows a vertical to overhanging line up the arête, laybacking to a blank mid-section with a distant pinch. Started: J. Childs, August 2005.

First Impressions Wall

18 Black Stallion Arête
(see photo in color section)

10 Metres 5.10d ★ ★ ★

One of the best climbs for its grade in the region, this route is sustained, and strenuous for its length. Climb up the steep west arête on small holds with increasing difficulty. Follows six bolts, with a two-bolt station at the top. FA: S. Hamilton, S. Morgan, October 1994.

19 Project

10 Metres 5.11+?

Open project from the original Silver Harbour Rock Guide (missing from 2nd edition guide) is just left and around the corner from "Silver Harbour Dream Line" on the easiest (really the only) line before "Orange Gonorrhea". Ascend the broken shale to solid rock. Climb up the steep arete on small edges, laying back at times to a thin, reachy crux two-thirds of the way up. Re-cleaned by Jarron Childs, Alex Joseph, August 2005.

ALEX JOSEPH

Orange Crush, 5.9 (above) and Black Stallion Arête, 5.10d.

ALEX JOSEPH

20 Orange Gonorrhea Crack

10 Metres A3 ★

This route is on an orange-coloured overhanging crack just right of "Black Stallion Arête." Nail your way up the thin crack and angle off left on delicate hooking to finish at the anchors of "Black Stallion." FA: J.C. Dubeau

21 Silver Harbour Dream Line

10 Metres   5.11b (or C1)

 ★★

A dream indeed. Crank the desperately flaring, steep crack just right of the first face encountered when approaching the cliffs on the trail. Or aid this route, at C1. The first

Silver Harbour Dream line, 5.11b.

recorded free ascent of this long gazed-upon aid climb was completed by a southern Ontarian, who is not convinced he was the first. FFA: David Smart, Fall 1998.

Derrik Patola on Iron Fist, 5.7.

22 Leaning Tower

13 Metres   5.10d  ★★

Climb up the flake and face to a traverse, then work up the crack, still using face features, to the top. The route follows two bolts. FA: S. Hamilton, September 1994; FFA: S. Morgan.

23 Lindsay's Big "O"

5.9 ★

Climb the flake and crack to make it to the top.

24 Will Power

5.9 ★★

Ascend the steep, thin start, to reach a nice crack and ledges that lead to the top. The first bolt is hard to clip. Follows two bolts, and needs gear to 3."

Record Body Count, 5.10a.

25 Iron Fist   5.7 ★

Jam your way up the beautiful fist crack all the way to the top.

26 On the Verge

5.10a

Climb the obvious corner, stemming when you can.

27 Record Body Count

5.10a ★★★

Climb up the balancy first few moves to a nice rest before tackling the roof. Follows five bolts.

28 Gale Force   V 2 or 3

In front of "Record Body Count," tackle the overhanging, five-move boulder problem. FA: B. Pullan, Steve Gale, Danny O'Farrellin.

Steven Gale on Greco, 5.9+.

29 Greco

(see photo color section)

10 Metres   5.9+    ★ ★

Ascend the finger crack to the block then negotiate the fist crack through the small roof. Gear to 2."

Silverline Wall

30 Reach Route

5.10a   ★ ★

Start up the middle vertical finger seam to the horizontal. Then move left to the first bolt. Move up from there to the easier finish. This route has three bolts.

31 **Flow**   5.10d   ★ ★

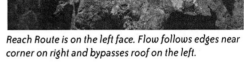

Reach Route is on the left face. Flow follows edges near corner on right and bypasses roof on the left.

Climb straight up small edges to the crux above the third bolt. Negotiate the tricky moves. Clip the fifth and last bolt and watch out for a nasty swing when topping out to the right. (It's easier to top out to the left). There's a two-bolt station at the top.

32 **Cliffhanger** *(see photo color section)*   10 Metres   5.10c   ★ ★

Start four metres left of "Mamba." Climb up the face and traverse left to a steep, juggy finish (four bolts). There is a bolt anchor at the top. FA: C. Davis.

33 **Return to Sender**   10 Metres 5.11+   ★

Climb the jugs to thin parallel cracks. After inching your way through the crux and into the small roof, pull the SLOPERS! There are five bolts. FFA: Brandon Pullan, Noel Gingrich, 2004.

34 **Cat Track**   5.8

A few metres right of "Cliffhanger," climb the fat crack in the corner right of "Mamba," using face holds, and then jams, to the top.

35 **Mamba**

13 Metres   5.8   ★ ★ ★

This was one of the first routes developed here. Figure out the beginning and you're home free. There are two bolts on the route, but you may want to add a small cam to your rack to protect the horizontal crack, as the fixed stopper has been removed.

36 Pullin' Out the Stops
13 Metres   5.11+ (or 5.6, A1)

Formerly "Stopper Lost," this route aided the first three quarters of the overhanging finger crack then traversed to "Mamba." Take the crack all the way to the top, staying to the right of "Mamba." FA: S. Parent, P. Dedi, 1982; FFA: Shawn Robinson, June 2004.

37 President's Choice
12 Metres   5.8

Pull up through the shale on the lower part of this line, to a thought-provoking crux move. This is a great rappel route, equipped with rappel rings to supplement the two bolts on the route. FA: S. Parent, P. Dedi, 1982.

President's Choice (5.8) follows vertical seam on the right of face. Cliffhanger is the on the left of the far buttress.

38 Ram the Big Cam   5.7
Use the face as well as the crack to master this climb. FA: S. Parent, P. Dedi, 1982.

39 Mashed Potatoes
15 Metres   5.7

Similar to "Ram the Big Cam," but more strenuous. Climb between two opposing dihedrals. FA: P. Dedi, Bill Ostrum, 1981.

40 Block Buster
(*see photo color section*)

10 Metres   5.10b

What seems like a stroll in the park becomes a nightmare as you traverse and mantle up onto a ledge. Start up the steppy beginning to an undercling/layback under the roof. Either mantle or reach high with a high step and pull on a thin seam to get standing. Work your feet up the face to a bomber horizontal ledge at the top.

Block Buster, 5.10b, has a wicked mantle, followed by delicate seam and face moves.

Great moves on four well-placed bolts. There is a bolt anchor at the top.

41 True Grit 5.8

That's what you'll experience is what you'll be as you tackle this gravel pit.

42 Boa Constriction

5.8

As a complete contrast from "True Grit," use good solid hand and fist jams to the top.

43 Short, Sharp, Shocked

11 Metres   5.10c

A grunt of a lead on an often-awkward line. Just right of "Boa Constriction," ride up the arête to a small roof. Large holds carry on to a small hand crack that leads to the top. This was originally a toprope route known as "Grasshopper." There are four bolts and a top anchor. FFA: B. Pullan, D. Hereema October 2004.

44 Made In the Shade

11 Metres   5.10c

This is a retro-bolt route named "The Ant" (5.11d), which seems like a more appropriate grade for the route. Just left of "Who Needs Skin," start on a large block, to follow four bolts to an anchor. Use the arête to the right, with tiny crimps and side pulls, up to the reachy crux.
FA: B. Pullan, D. Hereema;
FFA: B. Pullan, D. Hereema,
October 2004.

True Grit, 5.8 (left), and Boa Constriction, 5.8. Blockbuster can be seen on the far left.

Short, Sharp, Shocked, 5.10c.

45 Who Needs Skin?

5.10d   ★

Climb the overhanging face in the corner, using the thin cracks.

46 Climb of the Cave Bear

8 Metres   5.5

This route is in the cave about 50 metres left of "Mashed Potatoes." Start up the left side of the big hanging boulder, and climb over and up the right side of the face, to the hole at top. FA: Ken Smith, F. Pianka, B. Konkol, 1990.

47 Climb of the Cave Bare

8 Metres   5.5

This route is also in the cave; climb the right side of the same big boulder, and then climb the right side crack, to the hole at top. FA: B. Konkol, P. Lemieux, 1990.

48 Silver Birch

10 Metres   5.10a   ★★★

Climb the up the arête past the second bolt, and have fun on the crux! There are three bolts in all. Belay off the eponymous tree.

49 The Unclimbed Crack

5.10b   ★

Climb the crack on the right side of "Silver Birch." The easy start leads to a short hard crux (if not using the next crack over to the right). Nice laybacks finish the upper half. FA: B. Pullan.

Silverline Wall, with Cliffhanger in the distance and Blockbuster in the middle.

Silver Birch, 5.10a.

ALEX JOSEPH

Numb Hypothesis attacks the dihedral and roof (center) before joining Stairmaster (right).

50 Morgan's Magic　　11 Metres　　5.8　 ★

Step up easily to a crack and start hand-jamming your way up the thing. If in doubt, use any face hold you find. FA: S. Morgan.

51 Ally　　5.8　

Climb the crack up to the dihedral and then do some stemming; all while dreaming about your girlfriend. FA: S. Morgan.

52 Numb Hypothesis

5.9　 ★★

Start in the corner, climbing a bouldery stemming start. Then work up the crack and right up the five bolts. This is a tough route for the grade; it might be more like 5.10a. Finish on "Stairmaster."

53 Stairmaster

5.7　 ★

Take the jug-fest, following five bolts, to the hidden hold at the top, where this line joins up with "Numb Hypothesis." This is a good warm-up route. There's a two-bolt top anchor.

ALEX JOSEPH

Positively Fourth Street, 5.9.

The exact location of the next two routes is not entirely clear. They are believed to be to the right of the large cave and of "Stairmaster."

54 Tumblina   8 Metres   5.7+

Climb the inward-slanting face to a small sitting ledge, then work the vertical face to a flake at the rounded exit move. FA: B. Konkol, F. Pianka, K. Smith, 1990.

55 Shrug It Off   8 Metres   5.6

Climb the large crack (squeeze chimney) around the corner from "Tumblina." FA: P. Lemieux, B. Konkol, 1990.

56 Black Hole

12 Metres   5.12a  ★

Rob Dynes on Mother Jugs and Speed, 5.10c.

This route is on the large black wall with a thin crack and a small ledge. FA: B. Pullan, Steve Gale; FFA: B. Pullan, May 2004.

57 Giv'er   5.7

Climb the crack, and use any face on the right if need be.

58 Positively Fourth Street   *(see photo color section)*

7 Metres 5.9 ★★★

Ascend the thin holds on the slab to a rest, before cranking to the top. The route has three bolts and a top anchor.

59 Mother Jugs and Speed

7 Metres   5.10c 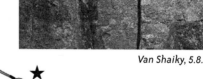 ★★

A short difficult section at the start eases off. Then comes the power crux finish. Has two bolts; have trad gear to 2.5."

60 On Your Marks

7 Metres   5.10a ★

Climb the arête on the right of "Mother Jugs and Speed." This route has nice moves, but is a little dirty at top.

Van Shaiky, 5.8.

61 Van Shaiky   7 Metres   5.8 ★

Climb the fun crack around the corner from "Mother Jugs and Speed." FA: A. Van Schaiky?

62 **Band Aid** *(see photo color section)*

5.7 ★

Follow the fist crack, using some small face holds as desired.

63 **Cross-eyed**

10 Metres   5.10c

Around the corner from Band Aid, follow the thin winding crack to top. FA: B. Pullan: FFA: B.Pullan, June 2004.

64 **The Nose**

5.7

Approach the roof from the right with visions of Yosemite. Then move left using small holds and a tiny crack that only Lynn Hill could crank.

Perspiring Buckets, 5.10a.

Sunnyside Wall

65 **After the Fall**   5.10a
Stem up the orange dihedral just left of the access gully.

66 **Bright and Sunny**   5.6 ★
Climb up over the bulge and traverse to the left. This route is a little tricky for 5.6.

67 **Sunny Side Up**   10 Metres   5.7 ★★★
A fun, easy slab with three well-placed bolts and top anchors, this route starts right of "Bright and Sunny." Climb the slab starting in the juggy crack, and work up the large holds to the top. FA: Brandon Pullan, Steve Gale; FFA: B. Pullan, S. Gale, May 2004.

68 **Well Done**   5.9
This alternate start to "Sunny Side Up" takes the left wall through a big reachy move to join the main route at the second bolt.

69 **Cam's Crack**   5.7 ★★
Start right of "Bright and Sunny" and climb up the crack to the top.

70 **Rec'er Revisited**   5.7 ★
Climb the distinctive hand crack, just like LU Outdoor Rec students have for decades.

71 **Paul Bunyan's Nose**   5.8
Climb the large crack any way you can.

72 Digit Damage

5.9+

Start cranking on small face holds until you reach the crack, and then start jamming away.

73 Blanchard's Buttress

5.8

Follow the crack over the buttress to the top.

74 Perspiring Buckets

5.10a

Start on small face holds. Then traverse onto the arête, using the faces as available. Follows four bolts to a two-bolt station at the top. Tough for the grade; better think of this one as a 5.10b/c.

75 Squirrel Slab 5.5

You'll just have to have a look for yourself.

Nasty Girls, 5.11a.

76 Winter Wonderland 9 Metres 5.7

A true walk in the park, and a nice intro to sport leading. Three bolts lead to chains.

Orgasmatron Wall

77 Frogs In the Blender 5.9

Climb up to the roof (one bolt). Once over it, move right to the crack and then to the top.

78 Rubber Arm Bar 5.7

Climb the crack and enjoy the feeling you'll get in your arms.

79 Temper Tantrum 5.10a

Climb the crack. Since there are no feet, use all the stemming moves you can find.

80 Nasty Girls 13 Metres 5.11a ★ ★ ★

This is a test piece and a real tendon burner. It's well protected, with five well-placed bolts and chains at the top. Going over the middle bulge involves a really reachy move from thin footholds. Since the 1st ascent, a small undercling has come off, causing some to suggest the grade be bumped up to 5.11b/c.

Sunset Strawberries, 5.11a, with Raspberry Belay in the corner at the extreme left.

ALEX JOSEPH

81 Christophe Project
?m   5.?

The next three climbs are located 25 metres beyond "Nasty Girls" on the opposing (east) wall.

82 Raspberry Belay

13 Metres   5.8   ★

A fun climb, this route is also a reasonable ascent to get to the top of the 2 sport climbs beside it. In the corner left and around the arête from "Sunset Strawberries" and right of the raspberry bush, climb up the corner, stemming on ledges, with some great holds and good protection. Descend via the rappel down "Power of the Claw". FA: A. Joseph, J. Childs, August 2005.

83 Sunset Strawberries   13 Metres   5.11a   ★★

Climb the arête just left of "Power of the Claw," following five bolts to a set of chains. Use the tiny side pulls and slopers until you get into the crack. The balancy crux is at the top. FA: Brandon Pullan, Steve Gale, Noel Gingrich; FFA: B. Pullan, S. Gale, May 2004.

84 The Power of the Claw   15 Metres   5.11b   ★★

Crimp tiny edges on the face to get into nice pockets. Reachy moves lead to the flaring crack at the top. Four bolts lead to a two-bolt station. Recent cleaning may have upped the grade. FA: S. Hamilton.

85 Nothing Up My Sleeve *(see photo color section)* 15 Metres 5.9+   ★

Ascend the easy blocks to a small dirty roof, then complete an awkward move to get to the top. FA: C. Jackson.

15 Minutes to Heaven

Well, maybe it's not quite heaven. But those adventurous to thrash about 15 minutes further east will find some fun stuff. The cliffs degrade, and then reappear.

86 Distant Travels   9 Metres   5.10a

In a hollow between some trees, climb the overhanging corner to reach a series of horizontal cracks and face holds above. FA: Chris Joseph, Alex Joseph, April 1996.

87 Cloud 9   15 Metres   5.10a    ★

This was a birthday first ascent. Take a high step out of the forest. Do the side pull and reach onto the face for a bomber ledge. Work up from ledge to ledge, and you're on Cloud 9! FA: A. Joseph, J. Childs, May 1996.

88 Abstract Brain Candy   13 Metres   5.10d   ★★

Step out of the swamp onto a large boulder to start. Concentrate on the arête (5.11-), but don't neglect a knee bar, or an occasional use of the cracks. Work the sustained edging and smears above, with some good reachy moves. FA: A. Joseph, C. Joseph, April 1996.

89 Bombs Away Petey!   13 Metres   5.8+

A bomber hold route that uses a healthy flake and the pointy corner. Pull the first move to a bushy ledge. Muscle up the bomber holds to the top. FA: A. Joseph, J. Childs May, 1996.

90 Assinine and Out of My League   13 Metres   5.10c   ★★

This sustained route takes the bold arête. A cruxy beginning on minute crimpers leads up the face to the right and then back to arête. FA: J. Childs, A. Joseph, May, 1996.

91 Bearded Wonder   12 Metres   5.8   ★

This overhanging route follows many odd blocks and small cracks. Take many small nuts. FFA: C. Joseph, A. Joseph, April 1996.

92 Block of Death   (see photo color section)   12 Metres   5.7

Work up the lichen-covered corner and avoid the terrifying block of death. Needs big gear to 4." FFA: A. Joseph, C. Joseph, April 1996.

93 Elvis Enroute   10 Metres   5.9   ★

This route works the face around the corner right of "Block of Death." A crux at mid-route leads to a mantle move, and you're home free. FA: J. Childs, C. Joseph, A. Joseph, May 1996.

94 Project   9 Metres   5.12?

The face left of "Huber" overhangs (~100 degrees), with a limited array of crimpers and sidepulls. This is the easiest line available, but it's still an assured tendonectomy. FA: J. Childs, C. Joseph, A. Joseph, May 1996.

95 Huber Goes To Yosemite   (see photo color section)

10 Metres   5.10+   ★

Find the orange-streaked thin crack. Working the face and some intense finger jams, levitate up the crack to some nice holds and rests further up. FA: C. Joseph, A. Joseph, May 1996.

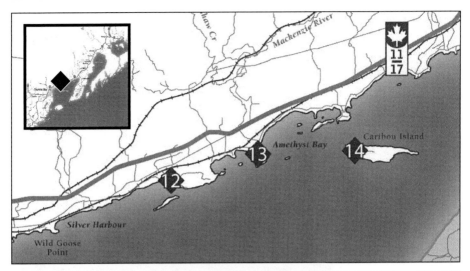

 **McKenzie**

Route Character Sport – 3, Trad – 5, Mixed – 2, Toprope – 5, Multi-pitch – 0

Route Difficulty 5.8 – 1
              5.9   1
              5.10   7
              5.11 + 5

Getting There: If access is allowed in the future, park along the road before the T-junction, so as not to disturb campers' access to the south. The trail has been flagged with blue tape on trees starting from southeast corner of the junction. The trail leads about 100 metres through bush, to the base of "Liken To Not Like Lichen." When you get there, "Short, Steep & Horny" is to the right (south). Or, once access issues are resolved, it may be possible to access from the east via the driveway.

This area is closed at present, though hope remains of re-opening it. The reason for this rock-lust is obvious; less than a half hour from Thunder Bay, the solid rock of McKenzie holds a number of steep difficult climbs, including a number of sport routes. There is clearly the potential for more hard routes.

Access Issues

This area is closed at present. Do not climb here. The area is private property, and the owner is a little leery about the idea of climbing. If we're lucky, access to these routes will open up. For more info, contact the Thunder Bay section of the Alpine Club of Canada.

History

McKenzie is a predominantly sport climbing and toprope area developed over two years (1994–95). It is an intermediate climbing area with many sustained, steep routes.

Camping

Check in with International Hostel; near the East end of Lakeshore Drive.

Swimming

There is good swimming at McKenzie River, west of the climbing area. Follow Beach Road west.

Broken Bike Bottom Wall

All of these routes have bolts as top anchors.

1 Short, Steep & Horny

11 Metres   5.10a   ★

Walk up a ramp to a ledge with a large tree. This little routes offers an exciting mixed lead, with a bolt to clip before grabbing the horn. FA: C. Joseph, 1995.

Rob Dynes on an early-season climb of Liken to Not Liken, 5.10c.

2 Tempting Chaos   18 Metres   5.12–    ★

A bouldery start leads to a rest. Then move into a very steep and crimpy crux, finally reaching a finish on the slab. FA: S. Bent, 1995.

3 Liken To Not Like Lichen   20 Metres   5.10c   ★★★

Start on the overhanging wall with six bolts, then surmount the crux on the technical slab above to finish. FA: S. Bent, 1995.

4 Soap On a Rope   20 Metres   5.10c   ★★

This technical slab allows some nail biting moves, protected by a line of well-spaced bolts. Climb up past two bolts to a ledge, then work left and up on thin holds covered by four more bolts. FA: C. Joseph, July 1995.

5 Unknown   20 Metres   5.10d

A tricky start leads to a steep finish on the large arête. FA: C. Davis?

6 Unknown   20 Metres   5.10d   ★

Start up the wicked finger crack, then traverse out right and finish on the large arête. FA: F. Latimer?

7 Riot In the Street   20 Metres   5.10b   ★ ★

Ascends the same crack as Latimer's "Unknown" above, but heads left through the bulge, past one bolt and to the top. This climb deserves to be a classic! FA: C. Joseph, May 1996.

Three Sides to Everything Wall

8 Secure Foothold   18 Metres   5.10d   ★

This five-bolt route will make you think, from its power-mantle start to the delicate, balancy finish. FA: D. Salonen; FFA: C. Joseph, July, 1995.

9 Plastic Mars   16 Metres   5.8   ★

This route starts left of the large flake and then works its way onto the flake to finish with a mantle move. Things get sort of runout at the top. Have gear to to 3." FA: S. Bent, 1995; FFA: C. Joseph, F. Latimer, July, 1996.

10 Finger Locking Good   16 Metres   5.9   ★

Climb the fine finger crack up to the ledge, and then work up the short face above the large ledge. Gear to 3" is useful.

11 For Maidens and Boys   17 Metres   5.11a    ★ ★ ★

After a reachy, power-crux start, enjoy the delicate climbing that remains. Follows five bolts. FA: S. Bent, 1995.

12 Forced Balance   16 Metres   5.11b   ★

Be prepared to think! Not only is this climb very balancy, but it will take some serious horsepower to get up the arête. FA: R. Dynes, 1995.

13 Unknown   17 Metres   5.11+

FA: R. Dynes, 1995.

14 The Great Green Anal Implant   20 Metres   5.11–   ★

This route starts up the pillar underneath the cracks of "Unknown" (below), but then traverses right to a series of seams. From there, climb through the overlaps in a crazy sequence. FA: C. Joseph, September, 1995.

15 Unknown   20 Metres   5.10b

Start in the corner and continue up using two cracks. Requires gear to 3."

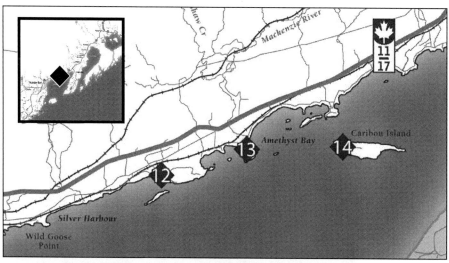

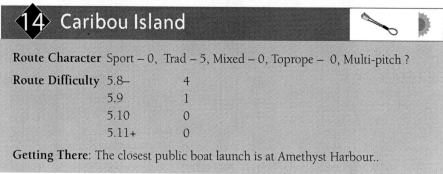

14 Caribou Island

Route Character Sport – 0, Trad – 5, Mixed – 0, Toprope – 0, Multi-pitch ?

Route Difficulty	
5.8–	4
5.9	1
5.10	0
5.11+	0

Getting There: The closest public boat launch is at Amethyst Harbour..

The vast north-facing cliffs of Caribou Island offer an opportunity for almost expedition-style climbing. A 15-minute boat ride or 30-minute kayak is the only ticket needed to reach a kilometre or more of multi-pitch columnar basalt exposure, similar to the walls of Devil's Tower.

Access issues

This unique climbing area lies on a series of columnar diabase cliffs on the western end of Caribou Island, high up in the large bay for which the city of Thunder Bay is named. The island is accessible only by boat from the boat launch at Amethyst Harbour. The island has also been accessed by sea kayak.

History

The north face of Caribou Island abounds with multi-pitch routes that follow continuous dihedrals. The climbing potential of the island was first explored in the summer of 1983 by Shaun Parent and Paul Mahoney. They were dropped off by boat for a day. During that one day, they managed to rappel several corners, cleaning loose rocks, and they climbed two routes. In 1992, the island was visited again by Parent, Joanne Murphy and Bob Porter. They did three climbs, lowering a climber down the wall to clean the route before ascending back up by toprope.

The exact location of these next two climbs is unknown, but they lie on the far right side of the island where the diabase columns make an obvious bend upwards.

1 Cornered

40 Metres   5.7

Shaun Parent brings up Bob Kelly on The Prow.

This climb follows a left-facing dihedral to the top of the cliff. FA: S. Parent, P. Mahoney, 1983.

2 Slip Sliding Away   50 Metres   5.8

Climb a right-facing crack to the top. FA: S. Parent, P. Mahoney, 1983.

All three of the follwing routes ascend the edges of prominent diabase columns about midway down the island. Several bolts were drilled by hand on the faces of these climbs for lead climbing at a later date.

3 The Prow   45 Metres   5.8

FA: S. Parent, J. Murphy, B. Porter, 1992.

4 The Sow   40 Metres   5.9

FA: S. Parent, J. Murphy, B. Porter, 1992.

5 The Kow   40 Metres   5.7

FA: S. Parent, J. Murphy, B. Porter, 1992.

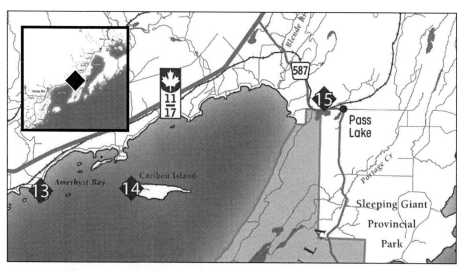

15 Pass Lake

Route Character Sport – 16, Trad – 26, Mixed – 0, Toprope – 22, Multi-pitch – 0

Route Difficulty		
	5.8–	18
	5.9	13
	5.10	22
	5.11+	5

Getting There: Take Highway 11/17 east of Thunder Bay, and about one-half hour east of town, turn right (south) onto Highway 587. Go south about 15 km. Park in the pullout across from Karen's Kountry Kitchen (which has excellent desserts and refreshments) beside the train tracks. Nearly straight north of your parking spot you will see the jagged crack of "Go Joe" in the middle of the Long Wall area. "Wild Child" is the large corner at the right (east) end of the cliff. Climbs are listed in order from left to right, that is, from west to east.

This is a unique area in the North of Superior region. The rock is steep to overhanging sandstone, with numerous layers and horizontal banding. This is a popular area of hard sport routes, on a warm south-facing cliff. Another attraction is great food at Karen's Kountry Kitchen.

Access Issues

Pass Lake is on private land. Climbers have historically been accepted by the owners, but have always been careful to tread lightly, pack out trash, and generally maintain a low and respectful profile. This tradition seems to have established a reasonable relationship in one of the more popular climbing areas in the North of Superior region.

Watch for trains around the corner! The fast freights through here take a mile or more to stop, and Canadian Pacific officials take a very dim view of climbers on their rights-of-way. In the past, they have made things very difficult for ice climbers in the area.

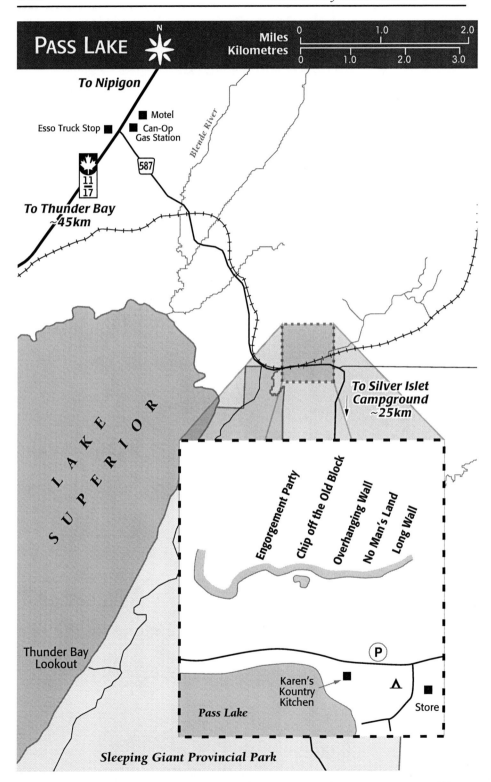

PASS LAKE

ENGORGEMENT PARTY

STAIRCASE WALL

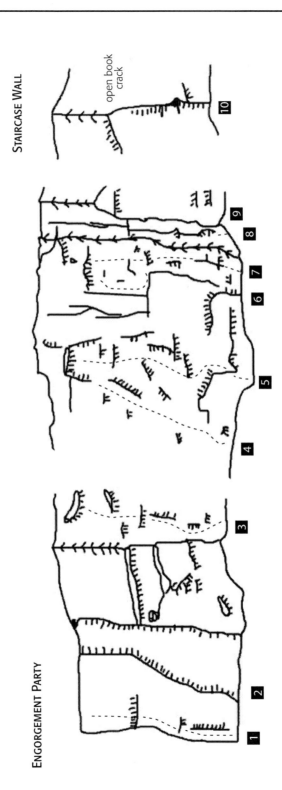

open book
crack

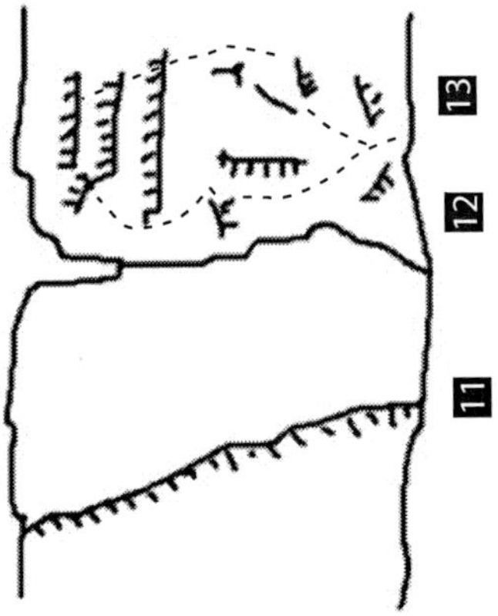

CHIP OFF THE OLD BLOCK

DOGS WALL

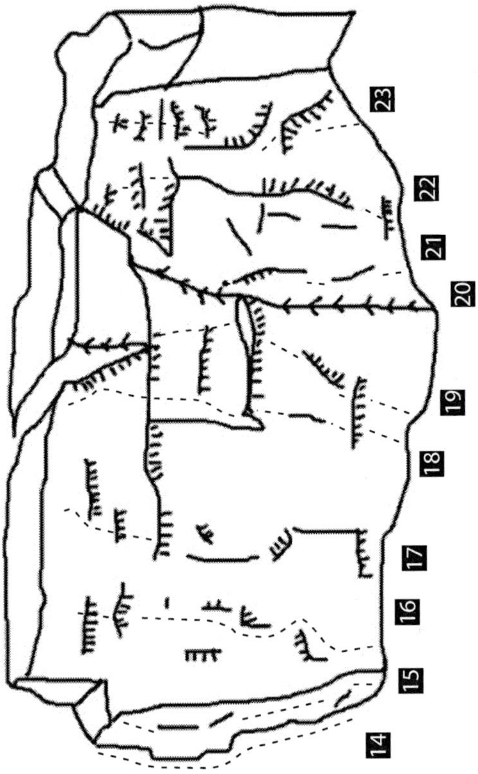

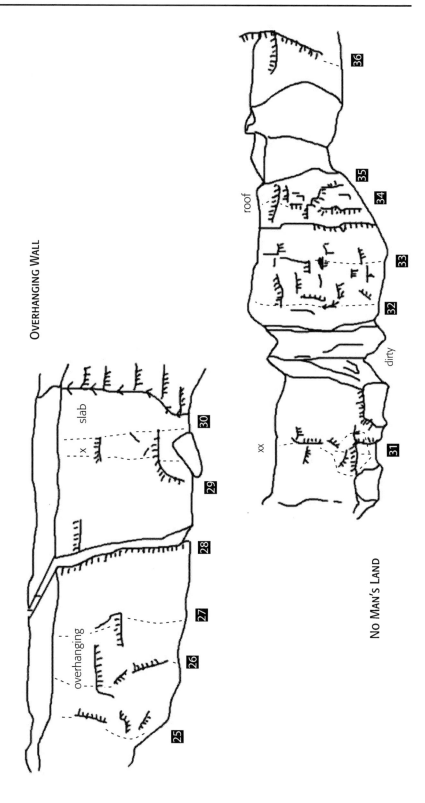

PASS LAKE

OVERHANGING WALL

No Man's Land

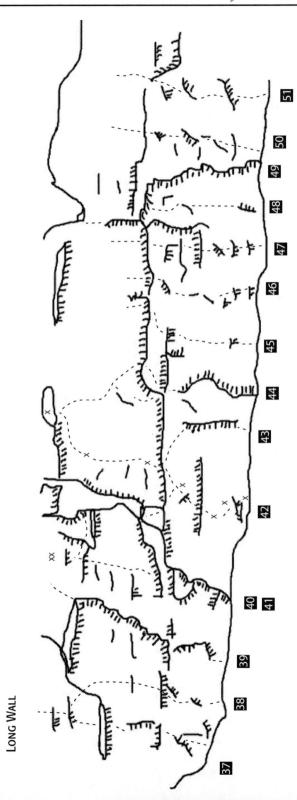

LONG WALL

LONG WALL

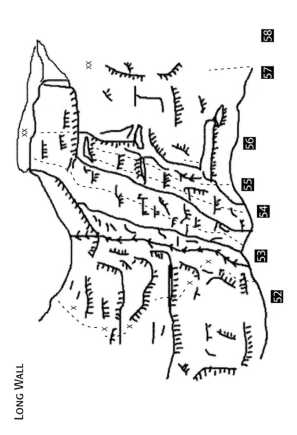

ALEX JOSEPH

Pass Lake is not hard to find. Just follow the desserts...

History

Helmets on in this area of lovely pink sandstone. At first glance one might question the idea of climbing these cliffs due to the talus slopes, but most of the routes are relatively clean and solid. But, let's face it, this rock is in constant decay, and you might pull something off anywhere. Pass Lake is unique in the Thunder Bay area as it is the only crag that the rock is not some form of diabase. The crag faces south and can thus be climbable on almost any sunny day of the year. The bulk of the routes were developed by Marc Barbeau and Chris Wrazej (and gang) in the 1980's. Bring lots of webbing (10 metres+) if you plan to set topropes. A rack of draws is all it takes to enjoy many of the new sport routes drilled since Spring 1996.

Camping

Pass Lake Campground is just across the road from the cliffs.

Marie Lousie Campground is about 40 km further south on Highway 587, in Sleeping Giant Provincial Park.

Swimming

The lake right across the road is good for swimming.

Engorgement Party Wall.

ALEX JOSEPH

Face Dancing, 5.10d.

ALEX JOSEPH

Engorgement Party Area

This is the area furthest to the west. The west end deteriorates into loose, broken rubble.

1 Engorgement Party   9 Metres   5.10b   ★

The western-most climb on the entire buttress is just two metres left of the striking rust-coloured wall of "Hand Jive." Climb the face and/or use the flake to get to the fixed pin and Onward Ho! into the crux. The exit is straight up from there. FFA: Marc Barbeau, Rob Hendriks, 1988.

2 Hand Jive   9 Metres   5.7   ★

Climb the wonderful finger/hand crack that splits the rust-coloured wall. FFA: Marc Barbeau, Chris Wrazej, 1987.

3 Unknown   7 Metres   5.8

Start just to the left side of the 4th Class walkup. Climb small ledges and cracks to ledges of lawn at the top.

4 Unknown   13 Metres   5.9

Left of "Heat of Passion" and right of the 4th Class section, negotiate the rough start and then finish on the slab.

5 Heat of Passion   14 Metres   5.10b   ★ ★ ★

This is a sustained and presumably once-well-protected face climb. Climb straight up the face to a small roof, pull through the crux and onto the thin face that remains. There is one old bolt still visible; when first ascended, this route had two bolts and a pin, with a two-bolt belay. FFA: Marc Barbeau, Chris Wrazej, Rob Hendriks, 1988.

Five Tendon (5.10a), is on the left.
Rocky Horror (5.7) follows the big dihedral.

6 Five Tendon

15 Metres   5.10a   ★ ★

About four metres to the right of "Heat of
Passion," climb the crack system to a large ledge.
There you can prepare for the crux, straight up
the crack and traversing right and up the face.
FFA: Marc Barbeau, Chris Wrazej, 1988.

7 Face Dancing

15 Metres   5.10d   ★ ★ ★

This is a classic face climb. Straight up the right
face, along the right side, and then cut left to the
crux. Move back right to the finish. This route
was recently retro-bolted. There are six bolts on
the route, and two bolts at top. FFA: Chris Wrazej, 1988.

8 A Ripple In the Pool of Insanity   15 Metres   5.9+   ★ ★

On the right corner of "Face Dancing," climb the crack system and stay off the wall to
the right.

9 Rocky Horror   12 Metres   5.7

Take everything you can get to make your way up the corner, utilizing the vertical
crack and flake system to the top. Looks better than it is. FFA: C. Wrazej, S. Hamer,
1988.

Staircase Wall

The Staircase Wall is a wickedly overhanging face, beginning after "Rocky Horror"
and continuing for 55 metres. The multiple overhangs make it look like an up-side-
down staircase. There is just one route on this monster.

10 Book of Dreams   12 Metres   5.9   ★

This dihedral is located two-thirds of the way down the wall from "Rocky Horror," and
just right of a steep ramp with bushes. Climb a blocky beginning to the crack, which
takes good pro. Finally establish yourself in the 45-degree open book finish. FFA: C.
Wrazej, Corry Zeigler, 1988.

Dog's Wall

11 Dead Dogs Don't Wear Plaid   13 Metres   5.7

Climb the left-leaning fist/layback crack with a balsam tree at its base. At the ledge

Rocky Horror, 5.7. (top) and Book of Dreams, 5.9.

Dog's Life (5.10a) and Pit Bull on Crack, 5.10c.

halfway up, either move straight up
(harder) or follow the crack left to
the top. FA: S. Hamer, Kathy
Gazda, 1988 (toprope).

12 Dog's Life

9 Metres   5.10a   ★

This route may be short, but is continuously difficult. Just behind a
large block, climb up the left side
of the face, using small holds. Then
attack the small roof. FFA: Marc
Barbeau, Rob Hendriks, Chris
Wrazej, 1988.

13 Pit Bull on Crack

9 Metres   5.10c   ★ ★

From the same start as "Dog's Life," enjoy a sustained crimpfest to a finish through the
small roof. FFA: C. Wrazej, 1988.

Chip Off the Old Block

*This small island of rock obviously
was once connected to the main
cliff. It is separated by the escape
ramp on the left and has a big roof
on the right side. The left side of
the cliff overlaps the right side of
"Dog's Wall."*

14 Praying Mantle

7 Metres   5.9   ★

On the left end of "Chip Off the
Old Block," climb the overhanging
corner with a reachy start that leads
to a tough mantle (crux). From
there, it's an easy but dirty climb up
the face to finish. FA: Paul Stone,
C. Wrazej, 1988 (toprope).

*Praying Mantle, 5.9 (L) and
Ode to Arapiles, 5.11b.*

Lichenstein, 5.8 (left) and Thunder Bay Transit, 5.5.

15 **Ode to Arapiles**   9 Metres   5.11b   ★ ★

Climb the overhanging face just to the right of "Praying Mantle." Sustained sloping holds bring you to reachy, crimping crux.

16 **Adrenaline Junkie**   12 Metres   5.10d

Just to the right of "Ode to Arapiles," head right through the bouldery start and crank the crux to easier finish. Dust mask is optional.

17 **Dancing On a Thin Line**   12 Metres   5.10a

Climb up the finger crack, then negotiate with the grass and dirt for passage to the top. FA: M. Barbeau, 1987 (toprope).

18 **Lichenstein**   12 Metres   5.8

Climb the face left of the spruce trees to gain a ledge. Follow the crack up to a large ledge and then out the top. FFA: Marc Barbeau, 1987.

19 **Thunder Bay Transit**   12 Metres   5.5

Climb the easy face from one ledge to another. FA: Marc. Barbeau, 1988.

20 **Self-obsessed and Sexy**   12 Metres   5.10a

This route is around the corner and right from "Thunder Bay Transit." Climb a series of thin seams and edges to the large ledge. Move left over the overhang and finish on "TV Dinners."

TV Dinners as seen from the road.

21 TV Dinners

12 Metres   5.9   ★ ★

In the middle of the wall, climb the left-facing crack halfway up, and then cut left up to the overhang. Dodge left out and around the overhang and then straight up. FFA: C. Wrazej, J. Carson, 1987.

22 Gourmet Microwave Food

12 Metres   5.11a   ♀ ★

This is the direct finish to "TV Dinners." The crux is pulling through the two small roofs.

Chris Joseph just under the roof of TV Dinners.

23 Binky Earns His Wings   9 Metres   5.10b   ♀ ★ ★ ★

Start left of the flake on the face. Work up and reach left to the finger ledge, the crux. Then trend right through horizontals, bypassing the overhanging section to the right, and to the top. The route has several old bolts without hangers. FA: C. Wrazej, 1988 (toprope).

24 Binky Right   9 Metres   5.10a    ★

Go up the flake, and continue straight up on rounded ledges (with rests) to the top. Not as exciting as Binky earning his wings. FA: C. Wrazej, 1988 (toprope).

Overhanging Wall/ No Man's Land

25 Dyno Mo 7 Metres 5.6
Climb the dirty face just right of the
walkup trail using the left-facing crack
and some rounded ledges. FA: Marc
Barbeau, 1987 (toprope).

26 Little Red Rooster

7 Metres 5.9   ★

Use both the right and left cracks up to
small roof. Pull it, and then traverse right
under the second roof to the top. FFA: C.
Wrazej, M. Barbeau, 1987.

27 A Question of Balance

9 Metres 5.6

Monkey Meat, 5.10a.

Climb up blocks and ledges to the roof, then move out to the right and smear up,
cleaning the dirt off the face. FA: M. Barbeau, S. Hamer, J. Carson, 1987 (toprope).

28 Are Ya Cummin, Or Are Ya Bummin? 9 Metres 5.5   ★ ★
Climb into the cave and then work up the layback crack to the opening in the roof.
FFA: Marc Barbeau, Shelagh Hamer, John Carson, 1987.

29 Baboons In Heat

9 Metres 5.9   ★

Crank the first roof, then power up the
face to the second roof. The route has two
bolts. FFA: R. Hendriks, C. Wrazej, 1988.

30 Monkey Meat

9 Metres 5.10a

Climb straight up the face. A harder start
uses a finger crack to the right (5.10b) to
the top. FFA: R. Hendriks, C. Wrazej,
1988. FFA: (variation) C. Wrazej, 1988.

31 Cave Crawler
(see photo in color section)

13 Metres 5.7   ★ ★

Climb left and out of the cave, using the
block. Then make your way up the face

Cave Crawler, 5.7.

Long Wall as seen from the Karen's Kountry Kitchen. Go Joe (5.7) follows the crack line on the right side of the tall face.

with a series of side pulls. Several options are available along this six-bolt line, from 5.7 to 5.8+. There are two bolts at the top. Variation 1: Muscle up and out of the cave, then straight up the middle (5.11d). Variation 2: Pull up and right out of cave (5.10c).

32 Crank'n In the Shade   9 Metres   5.8   ★

This route is around the corner to the right of "Monkey Meat" on the first face. Climb an array of ledges and small cracks with side pulls.

33 Knobbly Road   12 Metres   5.6   ★★

Just to the right of "Crank'n In the Shade," follow the rusty pink wall up a crack and then to the top.

34 Unknown   13 Metres   5.10?

Climb the sizable flake up under the roof, and traverse to the left to bypass the roof.

35 Dustbuster   13 Metres   5.10

A few feet to the right of "Unknown." Head up the face using a series of side pulls until you reach the 1st roof, then pray and crank both roofs. Black and Decker makes the right accessory gear for this route. FA: S. Bent, Mike Holowaty.

36 Trans-Siberian Traverse   9 Metres   5.7, A2   ★★

Starting by the spruce tree, climb the face to the right-facing aid crack above. FFA: C. Wrazej, Brian McCutcheon, 1988.

Long Wall

37 Manky Little Blade

14 Metres   5.7

Just right of the large boulder, work up the face to
a thin seam and then onto a ledge. Climb the face
above to the top.

38 Hidden Treasures

14 Metres   5.10c   ★ ★

This is the bouldery version of "Manky Little
Blade." Start five feet to the right, and put together an intricate series of moves to make it to the
halfway mark, then finish on "Manky."

39 Unfinished Symphony

15 Metres   5.11–   ★ ★ ★

This climb, located 7 metres right of the scree
ramp, begins with a tricky boulder start (two
bolts), which leads up to a thin vertical crack. The
first crux is getting off the ground; the second is
about 5 metres up, when the thin crack fades out
and continues as a wider finger crack about three
feet higher. Follow the finger/hand crack straight
up (5.7) and exit above. FA: Snell & Robinson, 1989; FFA: A local Finn in early 90's?

ALEX JOSEPH

Brian Kotyluk flashes Go Joe, 5.7, in sandals.

CHRIS JOSEPH

*Alex Joseph on
Go Joe, 5.7,
Christmas Day,
1994.*

40 Go Joe Direct
(see photo in color section)

18 Metres   5.9+   ★ ★

Start in the crack, but once on the first
ledge, move to the left and muscle through
the roof. Climb the face above to the top
anchors.

41 Go Joe *(see photo in color section)*

18 Metres   5.7    ★ ★ ★

Here's a choice lead and a pleasant climb
for its grade, with a cruxy midsection. It
takes good pro throughout, but have some
gear to three inches. Follow the classic
crack to top anchors. FA: Tom Morrissey,
J. Murphy-Parent, 1982.

Fear of Falling, (5.10a) roof on the right, with Go Joe roof crack on the left.

Paul Dedi on the FA of Fear of Falling, at the time rated 5.7 A1.

ALEX JOSEPH

SHAUN PARENT

42 Snow White 16 Metres 5.10b ★

This is a quality route, but an intense lead. It's typical to pre-clip the third bolt (on the first roof) because of the sheer commitment it takes to pull through it. The route has seven bolts and a two-bolt top anchor. FA: Eric Furlotte, S. Bent.

43 Fear of Falling 20 Metres 5.10a ★

Take the left-facing crack up to the roof and traverse left to the large roof crack. Finish on "Go Joe." FA: S. Parent, P. Dedi, D. Pugliese, (5.7, A1) 1982.

44 Five Miles Out 18 Metres 5.10- ★★★

Climb the large, left-facing flake up to the roof. There are two equally difficult options from here; dodge to the left, or pull the right side of the roof and then work up and back left on the face above. There is a two-bolt top anchor. FFA: C. Wrazej, R. Hendriks, J. Carson, M. Barbeau, 1988.

ALEX JOSEPH

45 Unknown Pleasures

12 Metres 5.11+ ★★★

A test piece for sure, and the sustained nature of the climb will definitely make it worth the as-yet uncompleted red point ascent. Starting just to the right of "Five Miles Out," follow the eight bolts, and end at the roof, where there is a two-bolt belay. FA: S. Bent, 1996.

Five Miles Out (5.10–), follows a large flake up to the roof.

46 Everything Goes Green

12 Metres   5.10b   ★

Green paint used to mark the base of this route. Climb the easy beginning and then hang on through five bolts and a sustained crux. Collect some beach sand at top. There are two bolts at the top anchors.

47 Chinese Water Torture

12 Metres   5.11a   ★ ★

Just a few feet to the right of the green paint. A single hard move marks the first half, but the upper part goes on and on. The route follows six bolts to a top anchor. FA: E. Furlotte.

Everything Goes Green, 5.10b.

48 Angimima's   13 Metres   5.9

Start just left of the large flake, and climb the face to the top of the flake. Cut to the left and the top. Or pull the roof (5.10c)!

49 Boogie Up   13 Metres   5.4

Climb the flake to the left. FA: T. Morrissey, J. Murphy, S. Parent, 1982.

50 Jesus' Hairdo

15 Metres   5.9

Climb up the flakes and ledges right of "Boogie" to a large roof. Pull through the roof to the top. Don't forget that Dustbuster. There is a rap station at the top of the route.

51 28 and Clear

13 Metres   5.8

A few feet right of "Jesus' Hairdo," climb the ledges to the small tricky bulge and then on up.

Tyler McNabb on Chinese Water Torture, 5.11a.

ALEX JOSEPH

Flying Circus (5.10+) middle, with the roof of Wild Child at right.

52 Flying Circus

(see photo in color section)

13 Metres   5.10+    ★ ★ ★

Climb the white-streaked overhanging wall and traverse left onto the face. When clipping the knifeblade, a foot cam makes all the difference in the world. Even though this route has seven bolts, a judicious leader might add gear to protect the traverse and overhanging section. FA: S. Hamilton, 1996; FFA: (linked w/knifeblade) S. Bent.

53 Procession

13 Metres   5.8

CDHRIS JOSEPH

Alex Joseph on Flying Circus, 5.10+.

Around the corner from "Flying Circus," crank up the inside corner, then sail on up the slab to a licheny top with two bolts.

54 I Wanna Be Adored   13 Metres   5.9   ★

Around the corner from "Procession," start up the overhanging wall to the first roof. Traverse out left (total of five bolts), and finish on "Procession."

Will Meinen approaching the intimidating roof on Wild Child, 5.8.

BRANDON PULLEN

55 Steeping Beauty   13 Metres   5.10a   ★ ★

On the same wall as "I Wanna Be Adored," work the black-streaked crack to the first roof, then into the corner. Finally, pull straight over the big roof. The route follows seven bolts, and has an anchor at the top. FA: C. Wrazej (toprope), 1988.

56 Wild Child   18 Metres   5.8   ★ ★ ★

Dig deep in your bag of technique to make it up this stunning corner. The frightening roof is bypassed to the left on a delicate traverse, with a great hold at a far reach. Or the roof goes with a flake pocket (bolt) to bomber horizontal ledges (5.10a). Needs gear to three inches, but there is a three-bolt anchor at the top. FA: S. Parent, P. Dedi, 1981; FFA: C. Wrazej 1987.

CHRIS JOSEPH

CHRIS JOSEPH

Alex Joseph on the 5.10a variation of Wild Child.   *Wild Child, 5.8.*

57 Conan the Barbarian Wears Ballet Shoes

15 Metres 5.10c    ★ ★

Climb the face to the right of "Wild Child," passing a bent bolt. The route has been re-bolted since then, and has top anchors as well. An easier version, which has five bolts, uses the crack the to right. FFA: C. Wrazej, 1988.

58 Mike Project   13 Metres   5.9   ★ ★

Climb the fine bolted line (five bolts and top anchor) on the right of "Conan." After a sandy start, it's well protected, so let it go 'til the anchor. The perfect warm up for lead climbers.

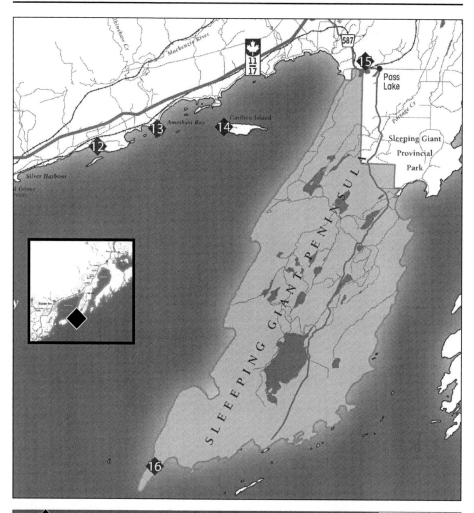

16 Sleeping Giant

Route Character Sport – 0, Trad – 23, Mixed – 0, Toprope – 0, Multi-pitch – 2

Route Difficulty	
5.8–	19
5.9	3
5.10	1
5.11+	0

Getting There: Sleeping Giant Provincial Park is at the end of Highway 587, past Pass Lake. Half an hour east of Thundar Bay, turn south on 587 and continue south for about 40 km. The park requires a permit. At the time this was published, the daily fee was C$10. Once in the park, follow signs or a park map to the Kabeyun Trailhead. Hike (1 hour) or bike (30 minutes) past Tee Harbour and Lehtinen's Bay. Head inland at the old Chimney Trail, scrambling up through the boulders to the base of the chimney. Do not use the old Chimney Trail, which as been closed because of erosion problems.

Jarron Childs enjoys the summit of Discovery.

ALEX JOSESPH

Climb as high as the highest gully where the bottom of the cliff on the left meets the old trail and a 50-metre cliff to the right juts out into the path. Go left here onto a very indistinct trail that follows along the base of the cliff for several hundred metres. You will break out into another boulder field. Continue left around the curving buttress of "Discovery" into the gully just below "Visitor Services" – this route is the prominent roof with two webbed belay stations. Work left (southward) along the base of the cliffs to find the rest of the climbs in this area. (The one exception is "Partners" which is to the right of the chimney).

This stunning location in a provincial park has a variety of routes (some multi-pitch) on some of the highest cliffs (up to 250 metres) in Ontario. Much of the long approach can be done by mountain bike. The park charges an access fee.

Although most of the cliffs have loose sections and some poor quality rock, the routes listed below are on good, quality rock. This area is an adventuring climber's paradise, but equipment thoughts should reflect its remoteness and the level of commitment involved in climbing here.

Access Issues

Since this area is a Provincial Park, access may become an issue in the future. Park officials are considering how climbers fit into their plans, but climbing is not a recognized activity within the park boundaries. Therefore, take care to climb wth minimal impact, and think about to whom those tales are told. The old Chimney Trail has been closed because of erosion. Do not use it as an access point above the boulders.

History

All the routes listed were done more than a decade ago and thus fixed gear is suspect. Since many of the routes were done two decades ago, a number of the bolts and pins are inadequate. Come prepared to upgrade prior placements. First aid is a concern being so far from direct aid. Helmets are highly recommended! Where the Kabeyun Trail runs west over "the feet" of the Sleeping Giant, another cliff face drops toward Lake Superior.

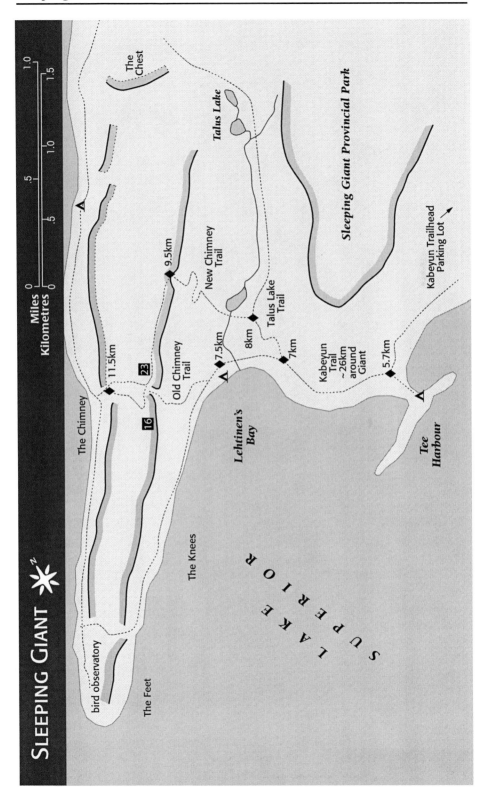

SLEEPING GIANT

Miles
Kilometres

The Chimney

The Chest

Talus Lake

Sleeping Giant Provincial Park

New Chimney Trail

9.5km

11.5km

23

16

Old Chimney Trail

7.5km

8km

Talus Lake Trail

7km

5.7km

Kabeyun Trail ~26km around Giant

Kabeyun Trailhead Parking Lot

bird observatory

The Feet

The Knees

Lehtinen's Bay

Tee Harbour

LAKE SUPERIOR

NICK BUDA

Discovery start

Top-o-Talus Area as seen from the boulderfield on the approach.

Camping

Marie Louise Campground in the park, has car camping. It is possible to hike in and establish a rough camp (minimum impact!) at Lehtinen's Bay or Tee Harbour.

Swimming

There is nothing better than finishing a long route like "Discovery" and jumping into Lake Superior to end the day. There is easy access for swimming at Lehtinen's Bay and Tee Harbour.

Sibley Top-o-Talus Area

Routes are described from left (south) to right (north).

1 LPH   25 Metres   5.7

This route takes the first vertical finger crack, beginning between "Halfway House Pillar" and "Lunch Ledge." The crack soon expands to hand-sized, and becomes a parallel-sided fissure. It joins "Psychic Wars" about halfway up. FA: S. Parent, A. Van Schaik, 1983.

2 Pyschic Wars   50 Metres   5.6

Begin on the far side of Lunch Ledge. Climb the jam crack in the corner of Halfway House Pillar and the main face. FA: S. Parent, A. Van Schaik, 1983.

3 I Zimbabwe   10 Metres   5.7

Follows the small roof and finger cracks about midway along Lunch Ledge. FA: S. Parent, A. Van Schaik, 1983.

4 Panty Lines

10 Metres   5.8

This route is a fist/arm jam crack, right of "I Zimbabwe."
FA: S. Parent, A. Van Schaik '83.

5 No See Um

10 Metres   5.5

Scramble along the ledge `from "Panty Lines" to Lunch Ledge.
FA: S. Parent, A. Van Schaik, 1983.

6 Invisible Man

20 Metres   5.3

Scramble up the chimney and large broken blocks that separate Lunch Ledge from the main wall.
FA: R. Freitag, 1980.

7 Dance Macabre

45 Metres   5.8   ★ ★

Just right of "Invisible Man," follow the hand & finger crack midway between Lunch Ledge and Popeye Pillar.

8 Whimpy

15 Metres   5.4

Start on the left side of Popeye Pillar and climb the chimney behind the pillar. FA: L. Jones, S. Parent, 1983.

9 Popeye

15 Metres   5.5

Climb the dihedral that starts just right of "Whimpy." FA: S. Parent, L Jones, 1983.

Shaun Parent on FA of LPH.

Looking down Whimpy, 5.4.

Shaun Parent and Andrew Van Schaik on the FA of Visitor Services, 5.6 A2.

10 Olive Oyl

15 Metres   5.6

Follow the fine finger cracks up amongst broken blocks. FA: S. Parent, L. Jones, 1983.

11 Brutus

15 Metres   5.8

Follow the first crack on right side of Popeye Pillar. FA: S. Parent, Uli Hoelinger, 1983.

12 Sweet Pea

20 Metres   5.1

This scambling line down the series of ledges is the descent route from the top of the Popeye Pillar.

13 Visitor Services
25 Metres   5.10b or 5.6, A2

 ★ ★ ★

From inside the curved chimney, scramble up a series of ledges to the big ledge under a monstrous roof. Climb or aid up under the roof and out right to a hanging belay. The original route ended here, but one can continue up the flake to the tree on the ledge above. There have been at least two ascents of this upper section. FA: S. Parent, A. Van Schaik, 1983; FFA: J. Bernst, Don Hickerson, (onsight) 1996.

Shaun Parent at the bivy ledge on the FA of Visitor Services.

An early ascent at the Sleeping Giant.

14 Up and Over Easy

(3 pitches)

100 Metres   5.7, A2

Climb the long, curving chimney,
(Pitch 1) staying to the right side
of the roof. Aid through the roof
and a series of deep grooves.
Climb finger cracks to tree.
Pitches two and three continue
directly up the face staying close
to left wall. FA: S. Parent, Randy
Frietag, 1980.

15 Jody's Butterfly

30 Metres   5.9 or A1

Begin on "Up and Over Easy," but
about one-quarter of the way up
the chimney, traverse along a sloping ledge to the right and into the
dihedral with bolt holes. Climb up
the thin crack to a flake, traverse
across the sloping ledge with a
bolt. Work up a very thin crack to
belay in the corner, and rappel from there. FA: S. Parent, J. Murphy-Parent, 1983.

16 **Discovery** (5 pitches)   130 Metres   III, 5.7   ★ ★ ★

This route is a classic because of its location, size, and the incredible view on the route
and especially from the "summit." It is the best (and probably the only) "alpine" route
in the province. The climbing is easy, but continuously interesting, with loads of protection. Note also that the potential for new routes in this area is staggering!

Start in the gully just below "Visitor Services." The start up higher, through a piton
and a bolt, is the route "Jody's Butterfly." The pitches as identified may be run together
(1 & 2 or 2 & 3) although due to wandering nature of route, long pitches may develop serious problems with rope drag.

Pitch 1: (20 metres, 5.5). Scramble up ledges from the mouth of the wide chimney
onto and up a short wall. At the cedar tree, in a flake/crack system, set up a gear belay.

Pitch 2: (20 metres, 5.7) Layback the prominent flake (on the right, with an old large
bong/piton) or climb the left flake with a harder mantle. Traverse left along a sloping
ledge, and lead up the slabby finger crack. Step left on the face to a belay with three
old bolts and pitons, in the corner on the left side of a vertical fist crack.

Pitch 3: (20 metres, 5.7) Follow the fist crack. It's easy going, but if you want pro
you'll need to slam in a bong or throw in a big (4" or bigger) cam. Work out over the

SLEEPING GIANT

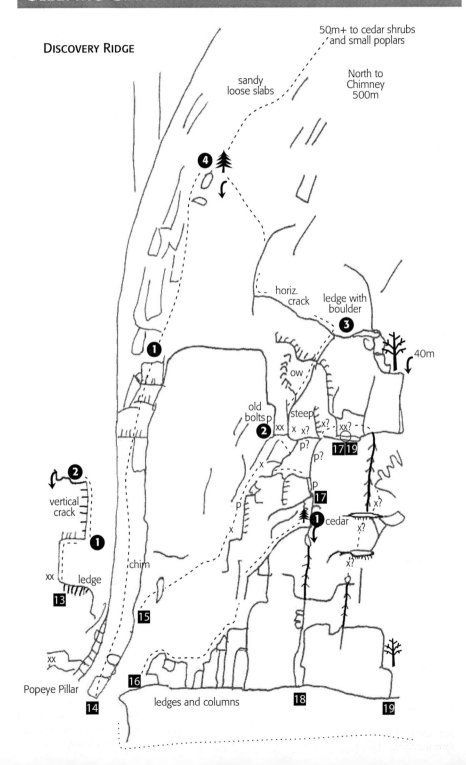

DISCOVERY RIDGE

50m+ to cedar shrubs
and small poplars

North to
Chimney
500m

sandy
loose slabs

❹

horiz.
crack

ledge with
boulder

❸

40m

ow

old
bolts p

steep

❷ xx   x   x?   x? xx?

17 19

p?

p?

x

p

❷

17

vertical
crack

p

❶ cedar

x?

❶

x?

x

x?

xx   ledge

chim

x?

13

15

xx

16

Popeye Pillar

14   ledges and columns   18   19

SLEEPING GIANT

SLEEPING GIANT – NORTH

Right: Discovery Ridge on the approach along the cliffs. First belay is in the middle of the picture where the tree protrudes out from the ridge.

Top left: Sleeping Giant Peninsula as viewed from atop Mt. McKay. Top right: Sleeping Giant Chimney area with the location of the route Partners to the right. Middle Left: View of the cliffs approaching the boulderfield. Discovery Ridge is at middle left. Above right: The tremendous roof on Visitor Services. Discovery starts just to the right of the picture.

roof and up to a rough ledge with some loose large boulders. Set a belay at the wall.

Pitch 4: (30 metres, 5.6) Traverse left around the corner along a grassy edge, then move up (several options) on some hollow flakes to belay at the cedar tree.

Pitch 5: (40 metres, 5.0). Continue on the left face to the corner, or work up the right face. This looks like Fourth Class terrain, but it is extremely loose and sandy. Hip belay or belay off of the largest poplar tree. Enjoy the view!

Descent: Follow the trail north along the cliff face for 200+ metres down and (eventually) through the brush, until you meet a major trail, which then leads north and quickly meets the upper chimney. Don't get climbers in trouble for causing erosion; do NOT use the Chimney Gully. FA: S. Parent, T. Morrissey, 1982.

17 Freak Show   20 Metres   5.9, A1

From the belay at the top of Pitch one on "Discovery," follow the fist crack found directly to right of the flake, to the headwall. Traverse right across the face and around corner to a pair of rappel bolts. FA: S. Parent, Barry Bingeman, 1983.

18 Obscured by Clouds   20 Metres   5.5

Starting at base of Cedar Pillar, ascend broken blocks and the right dihedral directly to the cedar tree on the top. FA: S. Parent, U. Hoenlinger, 1983.

19 Centaurian Travels   35 Metres   5.9, A1

From the ledge near the spruce tree, climb the dihedral to the top of a pillar with a loose block on top. Climb straight up a face and ledge protected by bolts, and aid up the thin crack to a wide ledge. Climb the thin finger dihedral to the ledge and the belay bolts at the top of "Freak Show." FA: S. Parent, J. Murphy-Parent, A. Van Schaik, 1984.

20 Yankee Doodle   15 Metres   5.8

This line takes the fine finger crack on the central section of Block Buttress. A fixed Saddlewedge is jammed into place at 15 metres. FA: Ed Kim, S. Parent, 1983.

21 Handful of Dust   15 Metres   5.8

This finger crack that becomes hand-sized is found on left side of the round pillar.

22 Bongs Away   40 Metres   5.5

This route lies in the first long corner left of the big chimney. It is poorly protected and has plenty of loose rock. Begin by climbing up ledges to a vertical corner. Ascend the corner to trees on top. FA: Neil Gilson, Jean Robillard, 1983.

The next route is right of the chimney.

23 Partners   45 Metres   5.6

Named for a big-wall climbing dog. This route follows loose talus to a small tree, then goes up the finger cracks to the base of the vertical wall. FA: R. Freitag, S. Parent, J. Murphy-Parent, 1980.

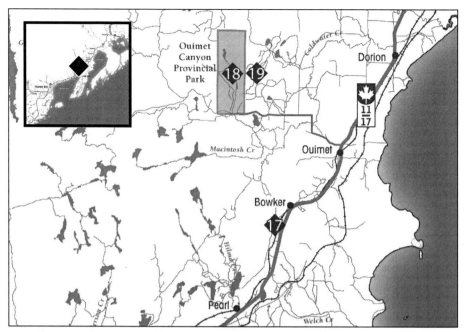

 Pearl

Route Character Sport 0; Trad 1; Mixed – 0, Toprope – 11, Multi-pitch – 0

Route Difficulty

5.--	8
5.9	2
5.10	2
5.11+	0

Getting There: About 50 km east of Thunder Bay, or 27.6 km east of Amethyst Harbour Rd., the highway slips through a rockcut that has an attractive pink face on the north side. Four sets of newer bolts on top indicate good toprope sites for easy face climbing (bring webbing). This a good place for intermediate-level top roping on slabby faces (uncommon in the Thunder Bay area). The disadvantages are the constant traffic, and the swampy base area. The belay area is typically drier later in the year.

The fine-grained gneiss slabs of the Pearl roadcut lie right alongside the Trans-Canada Highway. Although they are solid and easily accessible, they are rarely climbed. This may be because they are unusual for the region; the glacier-polished slabby routes are unlike any others in the area. While the immediately visible Pearl Roadcut has been climbed pretty extensively, there are several other faces in the immediate area that offer lots of potential for new routes.

Access Issues

Beware of trucks on the highway.

Tracey Gage belaying Jon Suazas on Dan Loves Brigitte, 5.9.

Pearl 1

Routes described left (south) to right (north).

1 Slab Dancing   18 Metres   5.9
FA: S. Parent, J. Murphy, 1981.

2 Smoothy   18 Metres   5.10?
FA: S. Parent, P. Dedi, 1981.

3 Dan Loves Brigitte   18 Metres   5.9   ★ ★
FA: S. Parent, P. Dedi, 1981.

4 Joey's Route   18 Metres   5.8
FA: S. Parent, P. Dedi, 1981.

5 Randy's Route   18 Metres   5.7
FA: S. Parent, R. Freitag, 1981.

6 Shaun's Route   18 Metres   5.8
FA: S. Parent, J. Murphy, 1981.

7 Ed's Route   18 Metres   5.8
FA: S. Parent, Ed Iwasa, 1981.

8 Honk If You Love Climbers   18 Metres   5.8
FA: S. Parent, P. Dedi, 1981.

9 Cars & Trucks Are Annoying   15 Metres   5.5
FA: S. Parent, P. Dedi, 1981.

10 Paul's Route   15 Metres   5.7
FA: S. Parent, P. Dedi, 1981.

Pearl 2

Nine hundred metres east, on the south side of the highway, is a large cliff hidden by the trees. There is plenty of opportunity for new routes.

11 Roadside Attraction   22 Metres   5.10+
Jam your way up a steep crack into dihedrals, which lead up to a roof. Traverse right and up. FA: C. Joseph, 1995.

12 Old Bolt Route   20 Metres   5.8
Left of "Roadside Attraction," route, start up a slab with an old bolt. Continue up through the dihedral. FA: S. Parent, P. Dedi, 1981.

Yet another cliff, the size of Silver Harbour, has been spotted one hundred metres west of Pearl 2, also on the south side of the road. There are also mounds of outcrop slabs one-half kilometre east of Pearl 1, on north side of road.

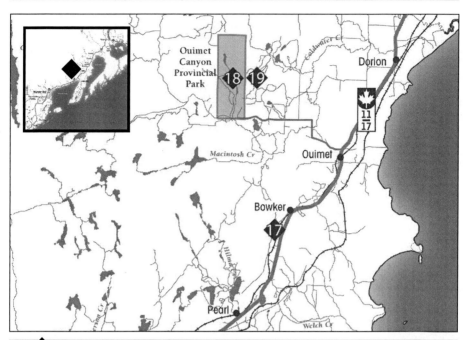

18 Ouimet Canyon

This spectacular canyon about an hour north of Thunder Bay, with its great views and spectacular formations, is a provincial park. The microclimate of the area supports an unusual Arctic ecology, and the Park has established guidelines for visitors to protect a very fragile area. It has been closed to climbing.

Access Issues

This park, about one hour east of Thunder Bay, is closed to climbing. There is no discussion about re-opening it. The following information is provided solely for historical purposes.

1 Indian Head

This climb has likely only been done once, both because of the restriction on climbing within the provincial park, and the remarkably tenuous state of the rock formation. This is very loose rock. FA: S. Parent, P. Dedi, 1980.

RANDY REED

Dorion Towers

Route Character Sport – 0, Trad – 7, Mixed – 0, Toprope – 0, Multi-pitch – 0

Route Difficulty
5.8–	5
5.9	2
5.10	0
5.11+	0

Getting There: From Thunder Bay, drive east on Highwayy 11/17 about 45 minutes to the road for Ouimet Provincial Park. Turn toward the park, and go 2.7 km to Valley Road. Turn right onto Valley Road, and go 1.6 km to a gravel road on the left that goes up a hill. At the top of the hill, park at the gate, and start hiking toward the Tower. Figure on an hour for the approach. When you come to the building in the clearcut, sight down the side of the building to spot the trail resuming on the east side of the clearing. Follow this well-marked trail less than one km to the top of the cliffs overlooking the Tower. Scramble down a third-class trail and across the boulderfield to the base of Dorion Tower.

Bryce Brown and Lydia Wiita on Dorion Tower.

BRYCE BROWN

Dorion Towers is, in all ways, a real "needle in a haystack" find, an amazing area of pinnacles and walls with steep crack and face climbs and great rock. The sleek tower just outside of Ouimet Canyon Provincial Park continues to battle with gravity. There is a lot of potential here for new intermediate and hard routes, as well as an incredible amount of bouldering. For being so close to the highway, it seems very remote and is rarely climbed. There great views on the approach, which is about an hour-long hike. A really worthwhile picture is guaranteed if you can arrange to be captured on the top.

Access Issues

There are a number of logging roads in the area. If crews are hauling, the trucks on the roads are all business. Park well off of logging roads and keep an eye out for the trucks.

The area supports an arctic microclimate and biome similar to that in Ouimet Canyon. Though this area, outside the park, is not restricted in the manner of the park, the guidelines established there should be applied here as much as possible.

Some part of the access trail near the microwave tower crosses private land. There have not been any access difficulties to date, but avoid any obvious impacts. There is legal camping just outside the provincial park.

Camping

There is a campground called Eagle Canyon just outside the park. It has two long suspension bridges which are spectacular.

The Canine

1 The Canine   22 Metres   5.6    ★ ★ ★

An classic route in anyone's book, and an airy place indeed. The block on top looks loose, but there have been no signs of movement in the past, so be brave! Frank Pianka took his son up it, so we can have faith in physics. The route works up a series of big ledges. Rappel descent is off of a webbing wrap. You'd be best to bring a knife to get rid of the old stuff, and to install some new material. Remember to leave your autograph at the top. Take gear to four inches. Double rope technique helps reduce the rope drag. FA: S. Parent, Peter Powell, 1986.

2 Planet of the Monkey Girls   20 Metres   5.5   ★

From the "Canine" route on Dorion Tower, turn around 180 degrees to find the big crack up the rounded slab buttress. Leaders will want gear to 3 inches. FA: The Girl Guides of Polly Lake Camp (toprope), 1997.

The Molar

The Molar is located alongside The Canine.

3 The Cavity   20 Metres   5.4

At the far end of the Molar, climb up the loose, blocked-filled chimney to the top. FA: S. Parent, D. Pugliese, 1986.

4 The Cleft   20 Metres   5.9

Climb the steep, fist-sized crack on the edge of the Molar, exposed to the deep gully. FA: S. Parent, A. Van Schaik, 1985.

5 The Filling   20 Metres   5.9

Directly across from "The Canine" is a blocky crack system. Ascend this, being wary of loose rocks. FA: S. Parent, E. Iwasa, 1984.

The Cuspid

The Cuspid is the long, narrow rock formation found close to the main cliff. It is a good close lookout onto The Canine and The Molar. The southeast face is a slabby face of rock.

6 Uli's Route   15 Metres   5.5

Scramble up the left slab to the trees at the top.

7 Mosquito   16 Metres   5.7

This route ascends a few short, steep slabs to the trees. FA: S. Parent, J. Murphy, Uli G., 1984.

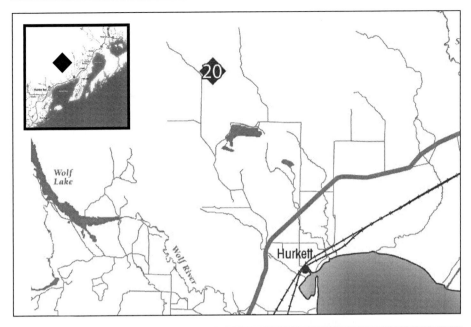

20 Claghorn

Route Character Sport – 0, Trad – 24, Mixed – 0, Toprope – 2, Multi-pitch – 0

Difficulty		
5.8–	14	
5.9	6	
5.10	4	
5.11+	1	

Getting There: Take Hwy. 11/17 eastbound from Thunder Bay approximately 45 minutes. 6.2 km east of the Esso gas station in Dorion, turn left (north) onto Black Sturgeon Road. Follow Black Sturgeon Road north, past a fork left to the Stirling landfill, and another fork left (5.5 km from Highway 11/17) to Stewart Lake. Just before the 9.5 km point, you will see a cliff on your right (east) through a clearcut. This is the Claghorn Long Wall.

To get to the Outward Bound Area, continue past the clearcut to the 9.5 km mark. Just before a bridge over a creek, on a left turn, park at a pullout on the right in mature conifer trees. (This is a good campsite). Total time from the city to the parking spot should be about one hour.

This is a rarely-climbed area of steep crack and face climbs, on great rock. There are many more potential routes here, and good bouldering as well. For all its remoteness, it is close to the highway and readily accessible.

Access Issues

Black Sturgeon Road serves an active logging area. Be aware of logging trucks and avoid stopping except on the edge of the road. This cliff is located on Crown land.

CLAGHORN

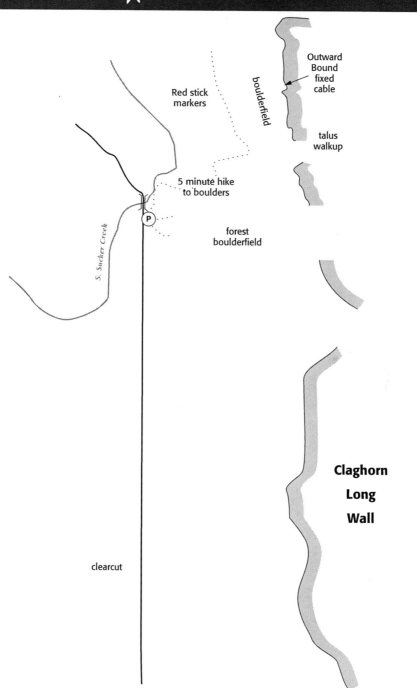

Outward
Bound
fixed
cable

Red stick
markers

boulderfield

talus
walkup

5 minute hike
to boulders

forest
boulderfield

S. Sucker Creek

Claghorn
Long
Wall

clearcut

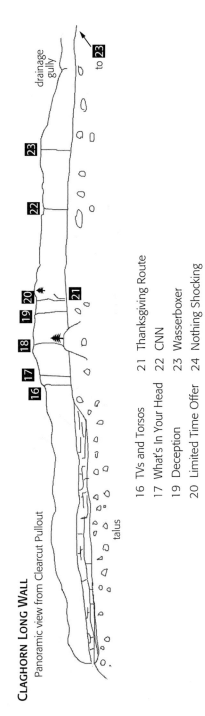

CLAGHORN LONG WALL
Panoramic view from Clearcut Pullout

16 TVs and Torsos   21 Thanksgiving Route

17 What's In Your Head   22 CNN

19 Deception   23 Wasserboxer

20 Limited Time Offer   24 Nothing Shocking

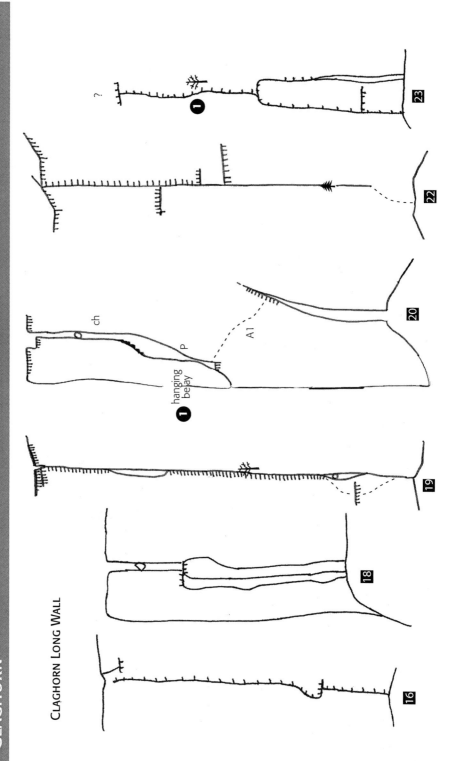

*Alex Joseph just past the
crux on Shakleton, 5.7.*

Outward Bound programs use these cliffs for their courses, so if you happen to be there when they have a class, have respect for them. But with so much cliff, there's plenty of room for all...

History

Claghorn: n. A mythical hairless, horny, squelching beast, believed to live among the talus. Generally recognized as the Protector of the Rocks.

Camping

Camping is OK at the parking pullout. Or, camp on the far right side in the clearcut, among some boulders, on Crown land.

Outward Bound Area

Follow the trail from the parking area through the trees and up onto the talus. The routes begin in a fairly condensed area, with a cleared base, roughly 15 minutes from the parking area. If you continue north along the cliff, you will come to a chainlink fence at the base of a cliff. This marks the bottom of "Faith," "Shakleton" and "Solstice."

Routes are listed south to north, as you would approach them along the talus at the base of the cliffs.

1 Flakey 5.8

Follow the straightforward crack.

2 Jacob's Ladder 5.4

An easy face climb.

3 Cracks of Dawn 5.4

This route takes the chimney.

4 Gendarme 5.7

This appears to be the face/crack right of the arête.

At the base of these next climbs is a fixed cable line bolted to the rock. There are many top bolt anchors spanning this area.

5 Solstice 5.5 ★

This route appears to be just left of the arête up a stepped, blocky corner that goes up through a steep section and a v-notch.

6 Shakleton 23m 5.7 ★ ★

This route is the great face route, to the right of a large, chossy, right trending fault line. It has been well-cleaned by extensive use.

7 Faith 5.8

This route follows the large right-leaning squeeze chimney.

8 Fairdinkem 5.5

9 Bridge of Sighs 5.9

Take the demanding layback.

10 La Connection Francaise 5.7

11 Ten 5.8

12 Raccoon 5.8

13 Fatman 5.6

A typical name for a typical chimney.

Northern Limit Wall

This area is at the northern end of the boulders left of "Fatman" and is marked by what looks from afar like a fantastic dihedral. It has a few faces that in some cases are remarkably clean and require only a little cleaning. At present, access is only by a bushwack path on top, making it challenging to determine where the routes are without a partner on the ground to mark the rope.

14 Pushing the Limit   28 Metres   5.10

This is a steep, long line with lots of edging, on a naturally clean black face that thins out in the last quarter. Completed to within a few metres of the top. FA: A. Joseph, J. Childs, July 2004.

15 Horny Finger   20 Metres   5.9

This is the easiest line in the last real alcove of the cliffs to the north. It's pretty dirty in the final finger crack. FA: J. Childs, A. Joseph, July 2004.

Claghorn Long Wall

The following routes have been ascended since Shaun Parent's initial foray. About 500-1000 metres south of the Outward Bound area described above is a new area first explored and climbed by Scott Morgan and Walter Mann sometime in the early 1990's. Beginning in 1995, Dan Green, Derek Moynen, Dave Duncan and Scott Fettes worked the area for a few summers. Ryan Treneer, Rene Lebel, Toby Harper, Brett Yeates, and Peter Smith continued to find and work out new routes in the late 90's.

The half hour (or more, for the south end routes) approach through the clearcut south of the campsite/parking area starts at a muddy pullout on the east side of the road. The majority of routes are located in front of the main clearcut block, and the last three routes are at the extreme south (far right) of the wall. For the first routes, walk through the clearcut, then through the buffer of trees and up onto large talus. For the routes at the south end, walk toward the wall through the mature forest to the south of the pullout and continue south over the talus. Go past a prominent drainage that splits the face, then past a monolith-like split pillar detached from the face. Continue to the area of clean rock and condensed, solid lines with a cleared base area. If the rock degrades then you've gone too far. Routes are described from the left (north) to right (south) when viewing the cliff.

From the road, the biggest blank orange face across from the pullout is the route "What's In Your Head?" It's easiest to find it first, then move to the other climbs.

16 TVs and Torsos   40 Metres   5.10

This route offers excellent clean climbing with good protection, on a direct and sustained line. Work up the finger crack in the left-facing corner to a crux, then pull through the roof and move directly into a nice hand/fist crack in an open corner. The finish offers yet another crux. Have gear to three inches. The route was named for the size of the blocks pulled off when cleaning. FA: S. Morgan, W. Mann, 1989?

Scott Fettes can't resist a Limited Time Offer.

17 What's In Your Head?

30 Metres   A3   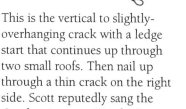 ★★

This is the vertical to slightly-overhanging crack with a ledge start that continues up through two small roofs. Then nail up through a thin crack on the right side. Scott reputedly sang the Cranberries song "Zombie" throughout the ascent to distract him from the rurp placements. FA: Scott Fettes, Dan Green, September 1996.

18 Shuffleupagus

20 Metres   5.8

Start up the crackerjack pinnacle onto a ledge. From there, work up the right-facing corner, into a large vertical off-width crack with a chockstone (which may be the only pro you can get in this monster!) to the top. FA: Toby Harper, Brett Yeates, R. Lebel, May 1998.

19 Deception   30 Metres   5.9   ★

Climb the face to a small ledge, then up a right-facing corner to a spectacular wider hand crack section, which thins at the top. The route apparently looked a lot easier on the approach than in reality. Take gear to three inches. FA: S. Fettes, D. Green, September 1996.

20 Limited Time Offer   5.9, A1

Start up the wide crack (have gear to three inches) that trends right. At the top of this crack, where it pinches off, trend left, aiding on the face over to a new crack opening up, that trends right. There is a fixed pin here, where the first ascendants did a hanging belay. Take the fun squeeze chimney to the top. The top of the route appears to be suspended, but for how long nobody knows! FA: S. Fettes, Dave Duncan, D. Green, September 1996.

21 Thanksgiving Route   ?

Starts up an easy crack in a hidden corner, with aid for the final move. The rest of the route to the top has not been completed. FA: D. Green, Derek Moynen, October 1995.

Shawn Robinson on
Ace of Swords, 5.9.

NICK BUDA

22 CNN   30 Metres   5.10a   ★★★

This route has been called "one of the best pitches of climbing in Thunder Bay." After a bouldery start, climb past a tree to a vertical hand-sized splitter crack. It becomes a right-facing corner with perfect hand crack straight to the top. This climb offers great protection on clean orange rock. The first ascendants chose the name as an acronym for "Climb Not Named." It was intended as a statement about the special wilderness character of this area, where there is no sign of anyone having been there before, and their feeling that they were exploring off the map. FA: S. Fettes, D. Green, September 1996.

23 **Wasserboxer**   30 Metres   5.9, A1

To locate this route, look from the cliff base out at the clearcut. Continue to move south along the Long Wall until you are lined up with the south side of the cut block. The route begins with a flaring off-width crack. Ignore it, and aid a thin line about one and one-half metres left of the crack, which joins the off-width (after it narrows down)

Shawn Robinson on Returning, 5.8

in a corner. Aid up another four metres, to where the crack becomes a flaring off-width with a tree hanging in it. Have gear to three inches. The route was named for Dan's VW, which he thought was a "Wasserboxer." FA: D. Green, T. Harper. October 1998.

These three routes are south of the prominent drainage gully that splits the Long Wall.

24 Nothing Shocking   24 Metres   5.10   ★★★

Starting on the perched boulder below the thin crack, climb through the low dihedral and roof. Then follow the beautiful fist crack (have gear to three inches) to the top. Descent is down "Ace of Swords." FFA: R. Treneer, R. Lebel, 1998?

25 Ace of Swords   23 Metres   5.9   ★

Starting 3 metres to the right of the "Nothing Shocking," climb the face to the crack through several roofs. Follow the widening crack through a short chimney section to the top. Rappel the route with a single 50 metre line, from the fixed slings and rings. FFA: Peter Smith, R. Treneer, 1998?

26 Returning   22 Metres   5.8   ★★

Three metres to the right of "Ace of Swords," climb the dihedral into the attractive fist crack, which leads to the top. Rappel "Ace of Swords" to descend. Have gear to three inches. FFA: R. Treneer, D. Green, 1998?

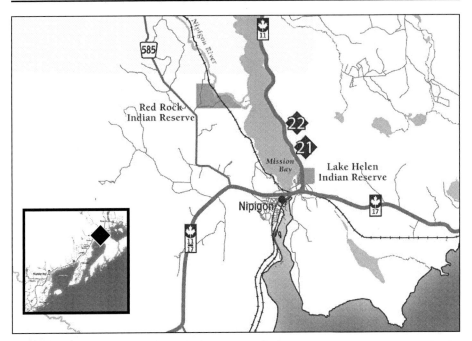

21 Mt. Helen

Route Character Sport – 2, Trad – 3, Mixed – 6, Toprope – 0, Multi-pitch – 5

Difficulty		
	5.8–	9
	5.9	2
	5.10	1
	5.11+	0

Travel   Driving – 1 hour

Getting There: Take Highway 11/17 east about 120 km from Thunder Bay, past Nipigon. About an hour east of Nipigon, Highway 11 and 17 split. Take Highway 11 north (toward Orient Bay), and you will spot Mt. Helen about 2 km past the Highway 11/17 split, with a small church and cemetery on the right (St. Sylvesters). Continue just 300 metres until the slabs are visible from the road, on the east side of the highway. (Chipmunk Rock is one km further up the road.) The vertical white streaks where routes have been cleaned of lichen can be seen from the road. A flagged trail to the top of the bluff winds its way up the left side of the slab.

The 70-metre walls of Mount Helen are a great, sun-exposed (SW-facing), beginner to intermediate multi-pitch area. The well-developed routes are conducive to beginning leaders. Even for the fact that it is accessible (with its 50-metre approach) and popular, it generally has a remote feel, and it's not unusual to have the entire wall to yourself. Look for blueberries on top if your find yourself in here in late July!

This gneiss slab offers beautiful views and great exposure. Many of the routes tackle short overhanging starts that open onto 40-metre slabs.

MT HELEN

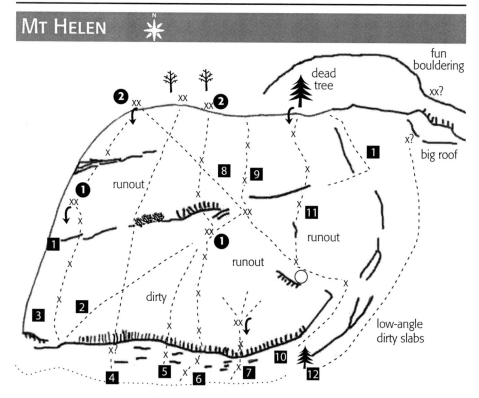

Access Issues

These cliffs are located on Crown land. Park well off the highway.

History

The cliff of Mt. Helen was first noticed by ice climbers going back and forth to Orient Bay in the early 80's. It was first climbed in June, 1984 by Shaun Parent and Scott Hamilton while they were working in Nipigon at an archaeological site. The "Standard Route" and the subsequent "Upper Dike" were climbed onsight with a minimal rack, while cleaning off the loose rock. Most of the wall was developed during the 1984-85 season, with a 5/16th hand drill used on lead to place protection bolts. In the early 90's, Bill Konkol and Parent went back to do "This Is Indian Land." In 1992, after a day of spring ice climbing at Orient Bay, Parent brought two climbers from Holland to the cliff, and they powered out two routes through the steepest section of the over-hang. In the mid 90's, the old 5/16th bolts were replaced by the Alpine Club.

Camping

Taj Mah Wall camp site, a bush camp site on Crown land that is frequently used by climbers, is about 20 minutes drive north and a five-minute hike in from the road. (See the Taj Mah Wall area description.)

There is a private campground and RV park about two miles west of Nipigon. With a dump station, movie rentals, souvenirs and a playground, it is sure to be an active place.

Derrik Patola on Bowels in Transit (5.7), with the Nipigon River behind.

Swimming

Swimming is available in Lake Helen (anywhere along the highway) or especially about 5 km up Highway 11, where there is a rest area.

Routes are listed from west to east, as one would find them on the short path (50 metres) that leads up from highway. There is orange flagging tape in trees at the highway, leading up into the climbs. For descents, it is best to rappel down "Bowels in Transit" or off the tree above "Overdrive."

1 **The Upper Dike** (2 Pitches)   90 Metres

Start on the left edge above "Bowels in Transit" and follow the most visible dike trending right across the entire cliff face.

Pitch 1: Start on the lower left section of the cliff, and climb along the groove made by the mafic dike. Belay at the 1st station on "This is Indian Land."

Pitch 2: Continue along the dike to the large overhang on the southwest corner of the cliff. Then turn left and climb to the trees. FA: S. Parent, S. Hamilton, 1984.

2 **Traverse Mercator**   40 Metres (?)

Start on the lower left of the cliff, and traverse the smooth face staying below "The Upper Dike" to end at the chains. Though this route is bolted, there are some long runouts. FA: S. Parent, A. Van Schaik, 1985.

NICK BUDA

Angela Pick on This is Indian Land, 5.7+.

3 Bowels In Transit (2 Pitches)   51 Metres   5.7   ★★

This is the western-most route with top bolts.

Pitch 1: (5.7, 26 metres) Start on the left side of the wall, just below a left-leaning alcove/crack. Climb up the face past two bolts, then over a depression (takes small gear) and up past another bolt to a bolted belay station.

Pitch 2: Continue up past a flake (more small gear) onto the face past a bolt, to a top belay. This route has rappel rings and is the best rappel route off the cliff. FA: S. Parent, A. Van Schaik, 1985.

4 Amstel   50 Metres (?)   5.9

This route is identified by the obviously once-cleaned (less lichen) path to the left of "Bowels In Transit." This route can be toproped from the top bolts or led. There is an old bolt below the initial overhang, looks dirty but used. FA: S. Parent, Ernesto, Martin, 1992.

5 The Dutch Overhang   40 Metres   5.10a, R   ★

Take a few steep moves on positive holds to a bolt, then climb up further through the lichen to a second bolt (5.10a, 6 metres). You can continue on up to the first belay station on "This Is Indian Land" (5.7 R) above, or lower off the sport route. FA: Martin, Ernesto, 1992.

6 This is Indian Land (2 Pitches)   70 Metres   5.7+   ★★★

Pitch 1: (5.7, five bolts) This is the clear ramp with visible bolts. To take the most-used route, clamber over the overhang to smooth clipping. Belay under the roof at the rap anchors.

Pitch 2: (5.7, three bolts) Continue up the licheny face to top. Rappel the route from the tree. FA: S. Parent, B. Konkol, 1990.

7 Freitag's Dilemma (1st pitch)   40 Metres   5.9

This route is similar at the start to "This Is Indian Land," but a little further down the way to the right. The overhang is trickier, though there is a hidden bomber hold, and a hidden bolt. It's smooth sailing on up to the rap station or the roof belay on "This Is Indian Land." FA: S. Parent, R. Freitag, 1985.

8 Ode To Rambo (2nd pitch)   30+m   5.6R

From the right bolted belay, trend up and left at 45 degrees across "This Is Indian Land," topping out at the second bolted belay at the top of "Bowels In Transit." FA: S. Parent, P. Dedi, 1985.

9 Overdrive (2nd pitch)   20 Metres   5.7   ★

Start at the bolted belay station right of the first belay on "This Is Indian Land." Go straight up to the top, supplementing the two bolts as necessary. FA: S. Parent, P. Dedi, 1985.

10 The Standard Route (1st pitch)   20 Metres (?)   5.4

Start around the corner to the far right. Take an easy bypass of the overhang, through greenery, up the ramp. A bolt leads to a ledge. Continue up to the two-bolt belay at the start of "Overdrive." Or belay on the ledge from one bolt and a small stopper in a corner and do "Neutron Dance" up the face above. FA: S. Parent, S. Hamilton, 1984.

11 Neutron Dance (2nd pitch)   25 Metres   5.8   ★

From the poor belay (one bolt and maybe some gear in the corner) of "The Standard Route,"smear and edge straight up the face, using three bolts, to easier terrain above. End at the tree on the right. FA: S. Parent, P. Dedi, 1985.

12 Slab and Shake (2 Pitches)   60 Metres   5.8

Pitch 1: Climb the low-angle slab on the far right of the cliffs up 40 metres, using small wires, and belay off a pin(?) and an old bolt(?) Note: these belay stations may not exist, or be usable, anymore.

Pitch 2: Climb over the overhang to the awaiting bolted belay. FA: S. Parent, R. Freitag, 1984.

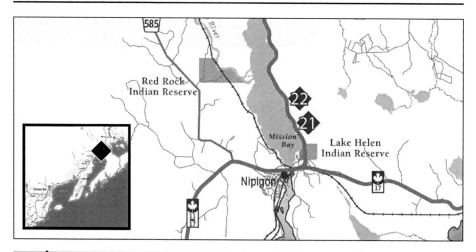

 Chipmunk Rock

Route Character Sport – 0, Trad – 0, Mixed – 1, Toprope – 3, Multi-pitch – 0

Difficulty   5.8–   1
                     5.9   3
                     5.10   0
                     5.11+ 0

Getting There: Take Highway 11/17 east about 120 km from Thunder Bay, past Nipigon. About an hour east of Nipigon, Highway 11 and 17 split. Take Highway 11 north toward Orient Bay. Chipmunk Rock is located about 3 km from this intersection, on Highway 11 about one kilometre past Mt. Helen. The short (five minutes or so) trail to the top can be found on the left side of the cliff.

This little crag (ten metres wide) has easy road access, and a small assortment of intermediate routes. It faces to the west, and is rarely climbed.

Access Issues
Not a problem; these cliffs are located on Crown Land. Park well off the highway.

History
Although it had been seen during frequent visits to Orient Bay, Chipmunk Rock was first explored in 1984, while Shaun Parent was riding his bike along Highway 11. He returned with Scott Hamilton, one of the archaelogists at Nipigon, a few days after ascending Mt. Helen for the first time. Shaun and Scott toproped a climb ("Highway Pancake") named after a critter that had met its demise on the highway below the cliff. The area was revisited by Parent and Paul Dedi in 1984, and they did several other routes.

Camping
Taj Mah Wall camp site, a bush camp site on Crown land that is frequently used by climbers, is about 20 minutes drive north and a five-minute hike in from the road. (See the Taj Mah Wall area description.)

Chipmunk Rock, with Shaun Parent's original route lines.

There is a private campground and RV park about two miles west of Nipigon. With a dump station, movie rentals, souvenirs and a playground, it is sure to be an active place.

Swimming

Swimming is available in Lake Helen (anywhere along the highway) or especially about 5 km up Highway 11, where there is a rest area.

1 Traverse, eh!   25 Metres   5.9

Start on the far left and clip the bolt. Traverse right along the sloping roof, clip the other bolt and go straight up along the finger crack to the awaiting bolts. FA: S. Parent, P. Dedi, 1984.

2 Highway Pancake   20 Metres   5.8

Climb straight up the face, past the small roof, and follow the sloping finger crack system to the left and up to the dead tree. FA: S. Parent, S. Hamilton, 1984.

3 For the Girls   25 Metres   5.9

Use the same start as "Highway Pancake," but continue straight up the thin crack to the bolts. FA: S. Parent, P. Dedi, 1984.

4 Horizontal Release   20 Metres   5.9

Start on the far right side, and traverse along the horizontal seam to join "Highway Pancake." Continue to the left and join the upper section of "Traverse eh!" FA: S. Parent, S. Hamilton, 1984.

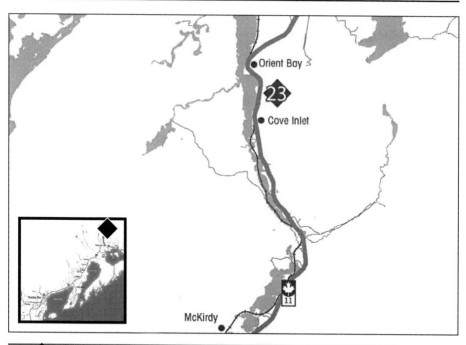

 Orient Bay

Route Character Sport – 10, Trad – 32, Mixed – 12, Toprope – 0, Multi-pitch – 11

Difficulty	
5.8–	11
5.9	6
5.10	13
5.11+	11

Getting There: About an hour north of Thunder Bay and just past Nipigon, Ontario (at the top of Lake Superior), take Highway 11 north approximately 39 km from the Highway 11/17 junction. When you pass a compressor station for the Trans Canada pipeline on the west side of the road, set your odometer. Go approximately one km further north where you will pass a parking lot on the east side of the road. Continue two km further along, passing a small gravel quarry and two small lakes (on the east side of the road). At the crest of a small hill, exactly three km from the compressor station, the highway begins to curve to the right. Pull off into the ditch and look for flagging tape at the top of the grass-covered embankment. This marks the trailhead. If you get to the Reflection Lake Cabins or the Pijitawabik Palisades pullout on the right, you've gone too far.

This trail provides access to the campsite, and most of the routes in the Orient Bay area that are not visible from the road. Taj Mah Wall, Da Projects, The Schoolhouse, and several small walls in this same area are all about 15 to 30 minutes hike in from the trailhead. Ice climbers familiar with Orient Bay will recognize this generally as the "Ice Palace" area. The walls along this trail are organized from south to north, as they are encountered hiking up the trail from the highway. However, the climbs on each wall are described from left to right when facing the route (north to south), as in the rest of this guide.

Please park well off the road! The transports don't slow down much on this stretch of highway! Head up the flagged trail and in about 10 minutes of hiking you will come upon the Taj Mah Wall; the first route you will see will probably be "The Colossus," with its gigantic roof.

Exactly one km north of the south trailhead, at a grassy parking area on the right, is the north end of the trail. If you are not camping, it is shorter to access The Schoolhouse from this end of the trail. To climb at Mt. Olympus, park here and walk north along the guardrail until it ends. Head down into the trees, and to the trail that leads up to the cliff.

Reflection Wall, Spy Wall and Mahkwa Buttress are usually accessed directly from the highway.

If you have any familiarity with Orient Bay as an ice climbing area, it will come as no surprise that this corridor is an equally spectacular area for rock climbing. The three dozen climbs listed here barely scratch the surface of a corridor that is lined with dozens of high diabase walls. This is an area of multi-pitch climbs, sport climbs, solid rock, and a lifetime of potential new routes.

Access Issues

The cliffs along the Orient Bay corridor are situated upon Crown land that has been reserved for recreational use. So long as no outrageous impacts develop, climbing here is accepted in a way that it is in few other areas in northern Ontario. The only major issue is to avoid the consistent, fast traffic on the highway; park well over on the shoulder and use pull-outs where they are available.

History

Although the Orient Bay corridor has been a destination for ice climbers since the 1980's, only recently has the area been explored for rock climbing. Not surprisingly, it is rapidly becoming the one of the best climbing areas in the region and is developing into an area widely known for the quantity and quality of sport, trad and multi-pitch routes completed (and yet to be developed).

Rock climbing at Orient Bay began in the mid-80's when Shaun Parent ventured part way up two routes just north of Taj Mah Wall, at the area now known as Mount Olympus. On a rainy winter day in 1995, Randy Reed and Rene Lebel discovered a mysterious Titon twenty metres up a splitter hand crack on their first venture to the Taj Mah Wall area. The fixed titon marked the high point reached by Charlie Farrow and Pete Olson during a 1990 winter attempt of the route now known as "Titon Crack." They had good vision; that 3-pitch route now climbs 115 metres to the top of the Taj Mah Wall and is one of the finest routes for its grade in the region. The following year, Reed returned with Martin Suchma to further explore the potential of the area and while doing so made the first ascent of "Survival Streak." In the fall of 1997, Steve Charlton, Ryan Treneer, and Matt Pellet put the first climbing shoes on the Colossus, where Treneer made an unsuccessful attempt on the headwall. His high point is still marked by a fixed nut. Reed, Charlton, Pellett, Treneer, and Greg Fedorak returned shortly after to establish "Rock, Paper, Scissors" over the course of three days.

In April of 1998, Reed and Charlton started a six month siege on the Taj Mah Wall area, joined along the way by fellow climbers; Pellett, Treneer, Lebel, Jody Bernst and Trevor Kenopic. Charlton and Reed returned to the Colossus and started up the initial slab; scrubbing lichen on lead and boldly placing bolts off hooks. Today this slab hardly seems to be the site of an epic first ascent, but the pitch was actually put up over six days requiring over a dozen wire brushes. In September of 1998, Jody Bernst made the first ascent of the "Temple of Zeus," doing the route in impeccable style as a ground-up on-sight. This represents one of the most ambitious climbing events in the region's history. One week later on a cold and wet November 1st, Bernst and Reed freed the second pitch of the "Colossus," the most sought-after pitch at the Taj Mah Wall. During this six-month effort, eleven routes compromising seventeen pitches of climbing were established. This effort also led to the establishment of trail systems and a tenting site.

New development continues, with Randy Reed and Steve Charlton (often coming from Toronto!) making weekend ventures, traditionally starting on Labour Day and going late into the fall. With a variety of others including Jody Bernst, Matt Pellett, Ryan Treneer, Trevor Kenopic, and Jeff Hammerich, they maintain the Labour Day Festivus for the Restofus.

New Routes and First Ascents

The style of the first ascents is noteworthy. All of the trad and mixed climbs were established ground-up and most of the sport climbs were climbed free when possible and/or bolted on aid, then led ground-up. Bolting was done on lead whenever possible. It is important to keep up this tradition both to respect the developers of the area and the ethics of climbing in the region.

Note: Do not bolt Reflection Wall. Given the nature of the spectacular ice climb that forms there, the consensus in the area is to leave the wall bolt-free. It is short enough that toproping is possible there.

There are a number of active projects here. Some are closed, and others are open to anyone that wants to continue the cleaning and development that has been started. For recent information on new routes in the area, contact Randy Reed.

Camping

From the south trailhead, hike in about five minutes to the Taj Mah Wall camp site; a comfortable but undeveloped camp on Crown land near the Taj Mah Wall in Orient Bay, that is frequently used by climbers. There is a rustic outhouse, but no water. Be sure to use the food hang to prevent problems with bears.

Reflection Lake Resort is 2 km north. They have comfortable cabins and friendly service. There is also a campground operated by the Town of Nipigon, near town.

Swimming

Swimming in Reflection Lake (west side of highway) is accessible just past the pull-off for the main trail.

ORIENT BAY

MAHKWA BUTTRESS
Northwest Faces

Southwest Faces

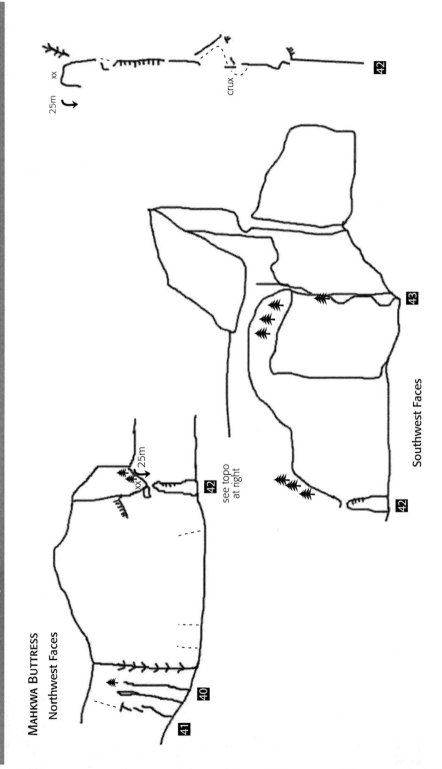

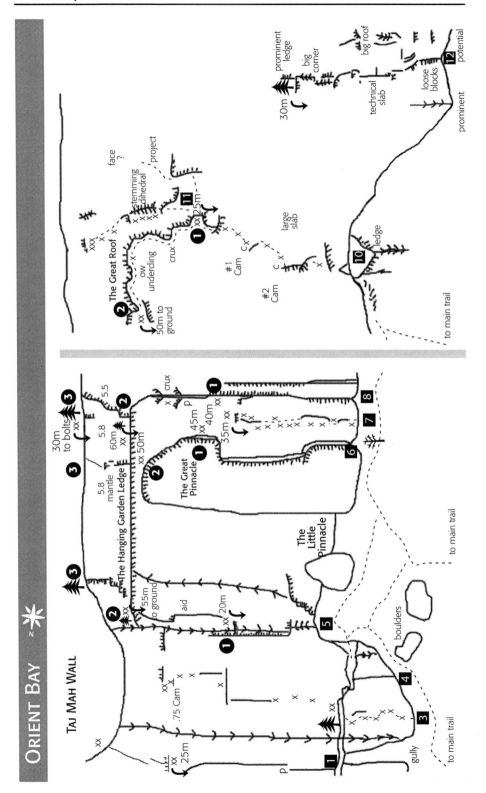

For a sense of scale, find Shawn Robinson on Titon Crack. The dark wall of Black Rain (5.11a) silhouettes the right side of the giant pinnacle and Temple of Zeus (5.10a).

ERIC LANDMANN

Taj Mah Wall

1 Qu'est-ce Que Fuck?
(2 Pitches)   45 Metres   5.9 or A1

 ★★

Pitch1: (5.9, 25 metres) Start from the ledge 10 metres left of "Survial Streak." Start up a discontinuous crack, then climb up and right to a fixed pin. Continue straight up a crack, exiting right to a two-bolt belay. Needs gear up to three inches.

Pitch 2: (A1, 20 metres) Not recommended. Aid the second pitch above on pins and stoppers. There are two-bolt belays at the top of both pitches. FA: S. Charlton, O. Lardin, 1998.

2 Funner Than Bubblegum   40 Metres   5.8R   ★★

This route is directly to the left of the second pitch of "Survival Streak." It's a quality route that separates the men from the boys.

Pitch 1: Climb up to and around the precarious flake, and then trend left on the obvious ramp. Belay at the anchors for that fuck route.

Pitch 2: Follow the undercling crack which trends right towards the top. Descend by rappeling that fuck route. FA: William Meinen, Andy Gallant: FFA: William Meinen, Andy Gallant, Spring 2004.

3 Survival Streak (2 Pitches)   48 Metres   5.11c    ★★★

Pitch 1: (sport, 5.11b, 18 metres) Wander right, then left, to an indentation. Clmb higher to the right and left again to the ledge. There are six bolts in all. Rappel off of the tree or climb up to a bolted belay.

RANDY REED

Matt Pellett on the FA of
Rock, Paper, Scissors, 5.8 A2.

Pitch 2: (mixed, 5.11c, 30 metres) From the bolted belay, climb an absolutely awesome second pitch by following edges and seams to a short crack. Save a TCU (consider bringing two) for the horizontal crack near the top. Work up past the crack and up bolts to bolted belay station under an overhang. FA: R. Reed, M. Suchma, S. Charlton, April 1996 (pitch 1): R. Reed (solo), 1999 (pitch 2): FFA: S. Charlton, R. Reed, 2002 (pitch 2).

4 Slim Pickin's

13 Metres   5.9   ★

Follow the crack straight up to the ledge. Along with standard gear to two inches, a couple of TCU's are handy. FA: R. Treneer, R. Reed, T. Harper, April 1998.

5 Rock, Paper, Scissors (3 Pitches) *(see photo color section)*

75 Metres   5.8, A2 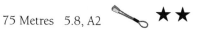 ★ ★

The route was named for the method the first ascent team used to see who had the lead each day. Take a generous rack, with extra nuts and runners, and gear to 3".

Pitch 1: (5.8, 20 metres) Start at a large cedar tree to the left of the little pinnacle and a big black water streak. Climb up the crack to a roof and move left into the corner above. Follow the corner until a small ledge is reached. A good hold on the arête edge to the right leads out of the corner to the belay.

Pitch 2: (A2, 35 metres) Move right to a finger crack with a short offwidth section. Follow this past several small roofs until the crack runs out. Climb up on the face past a bolt, and another small roof (crux). Continue following the crack, moving right to a large ledge and the belay.

Looking up at most of the 95 metres of Temple of Zeus.

*Jody Bernst mastering the crux
on the FFA of Temple of Zeus.*

CHRIS JOSEPH

NICK BUDA

Pitch 3: (5.5, 15 metres) Proceed up and right over ledges to a short corner, and follow this to the top. FA: R. Reed, S. Charlton and G. Fedorak, 1997 (pitch 1); M. Pellett, R. Treneer, and R. Reed, 1997 (pitch 2); S. Charlton and R. Reed, 1997 (pitch 3): FFA: M. Pellett, S. Charlton, April 1998 (pitch 1).

6 Temple of Zeus (3 Pitches)   95 Metres   5.10+ ★ ★ ★

The best of this climb was lead by Jody as a ground-up on-sight, making it one of the important climbing firsts in the history of the region. The ascent is spectacular, in that the route is intimidating to say the least.

Pitch 1: (5.10+, 45 metres) Start at a clump of birch trees below a beautiful, gigantic hanging corner, about 70 metres to the left of "The Colossus." Climb the initial corner using face holds and an occasional fist jam to a ledge and the base of the hanging corner. Stem and layback the widening corner to a roof. Finish up the flaring corner to the bolted belay.

Pitch 2: (5.10, 20 metres) This short pitch finishes the off-width and flaring chimney to reach another bolted belay. Pass the belay, and pop up left to the big cedar trees and belay there (so that second has a good view of the next pitch lead).

Pitch 3: (5.8, 30 metres) Climb the left side of the flake to a poorly-protected mantle (crux) before the top.

Rappel from the third belay station on "Titon Crack," 7 or 8 metres to the right. You need to downclimb a move behind some cedar tres to reach the anchor.

Gear: the first ascenscionist said that a half-dozen #3 Camalots would have been nice. Take multiple sets of cams from #1 to #4 Camalot; a #5 Camalot is optional but useful. FFA: (pitches one & 2) J. Bernst, R. Reed, September 1998 (onsight): FFA: (pitch 3) S. Charlton, J. Bernst, R. Reed, August 2001.

Black Rain, 5.11a.

7 **Black Rain**   35 Metres   5.11a

 ★★

The first ascenionist scrubbed the route for days in the rain. Climb the excellent water-streaked face three metres to the left (north) of "Titon Crack) up through 11 bolts to a belay. FA: R. Reed, J. Bernst, S. Charlton, R. Treneer, April 1998.

The face to the left of "Titon Crack" has been top-roped and local consensus is that it ought to remain a toprope problem. Don't bolt it.

8 **Titon Crack** (3 Pitches)
(see photo in color section)

100 Metres   5.9  ★★★

The first ascendants struggled with huge loose blocks, including the Refrigerator Block (marked below by the old titon) on the first pitch. This is perhaps the most obvious vertical crack line on the Taj Mah Wall, 100 metres left of "The Colossus."

Pitch 1: (5.9, 40 metres) Follow the hand-to-fist crack using some face edges, and muscle through the final sting in the tail at the finish. An easy jam in the off-width crack or a high step on the face gets you to the first belay.

Pitch 2: (5.9+, 30 metres) The second pitch appears from the belay to offer the same

Shawn Robinson on Titon Crack, 5.9.

Steve Charlton just past the smaller roof on pitch 2 of The Colossus, 5.11a.

consistent crack, but very quickly you will find yourself in a corner. Only a bolt (the manky pin that used to be here fueled a 25-footer when it popped) provides relief from this challenging set of stem/jams and pulls on mean little sloping holds. Later ascents suggest this pitch is more like a 5.10+. If the summit register is still hanging on the second belay, the top pitch hasn't been cleaned yet.

Pitch 3: Exit right on ledges and flakes (5.5, 30 metres) or straight up the slab (5.8) to finish in a dirty corner on a ledge with a bolted belay station. If you exit right, the rap anchor is hidden; walk left to the top of the

Randy Reed on pitch 1 of The Colossus.

5.8 finish and downclimb a move behind some cedar trees to the ledge with the bolted station. FA: R. Treneer, R. Reed (exit right out at 5.5), October 1998: FFA: R. Treneer, R. Reed, 2001 (5.8 finish).

9 Seven Wonders of the Ancient World (1st pitch of 3)

30 Metres   5.10, A1

This open project is between "Titon Crack" and The Colossus" on a 100-metre wall. The first pitch is pretty nasty, and would get a one-star rating at present. The upper pitches, heading left and up, look wild and intimidating, like someone took a monster ice cream scoop and scooped out a chunk of the wall. There are already a couple of bolts and a two-bolt belay station. Incomplete: J. Bernst, R. Reed.

10 The Colossus (2 Pitches)   75 Metres   5.11a   ★ ★ ★

This route tackles the massive roof on the Taj Mah Wall. The face below Pitch One has been toproped—please don't bolt it.

Pitch 1: (5.10b, 35 metres) Begin on top of a small block and climb straight up to a ledge with a bolt. Move up and left to a flake, then traverse right to another flake. Follow the flake up, then begin traversing right past bolts. At the final bolt, make an improbable move to the right, and blast straight up and over the small roof on the right side, on good rails, to the belay. There are six bolts, but a couple of #1 Camalots are useful.

Pitch 2: (5.11a, 40 metres) Take lots of gear for this long pitch. Follow the crack and flake up, and face climb with difficulty to the left under a small roof; continue up to the huge arched roof. Undercling left past a bolt and the second crux. Continue to undercling left, then step down to a two-bolt belay. Take gear to four inches, and include extra finger-sized cams.

You can rappel from bolts at the top of pitch one with one 50-metre rope. From the end of pitch 2, one rappel with two 50-metre ropes will get you to the ground. FFA: (pitch 1) S. Charlton, R. Reed, R. Treneer, M. Pellett, April, 1998: (Pitch 2) J. Bernst, R. Reed, S. Charlton, November 1998.

11 Standing Tall Before The Man (2nd pitch) 35 Metres 5.12?

This second-pitch variation is still a work in progress, a closed project. From the first belay station on "The Colossus," climb straight up the corner. Leave one end of your second rope tied on the first belay of "Colossus" as the rappel leaves you out in space past the great roof. FA: R. Reed (aid solo)

12 Greased Lichen   20 Metres   5.8

This dirty, ugly route is not recommended. But if you wish, start at the indentation/corner with a right-facing flake and some loose blocks. Climb up and then follow the crack that angles left and then up again, then work through a technical slabby section up to a big corner. Follow up arêtes to a ledge with a rappel tree. Bring gear up to three inches. FA: D. Benton, J. Hammerich, 2001.

Da Projects

13 Jump'n You In   20 Metres   5.10–   ★

Climb through the overhanging start and up the lightning bolt, around the corner (left) from "Jimmy Got Gat." FA: T. Kenopic, 2002; FFA: T. Kenopic, R. Reed.

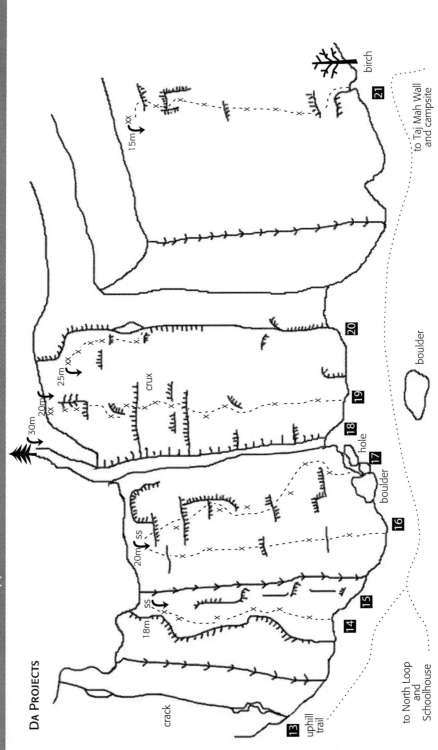

ORIENT BAY

DA PROJECTS

15m

25m

20m

30m

20m

18m ss

20m ss

crux

crack

hole

boulder

boulder

birch

uphill trail

to Taj Mah Wall and campsite

to North Loop and Schoolhouse

13 14 15 16 17 18 19 20 21

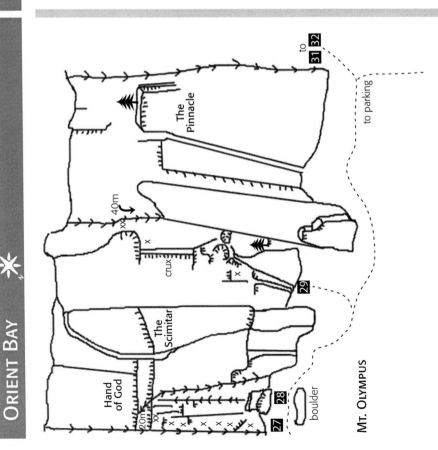

Nick Buda on Jimmy Got Gat, 5.10b.

14 Jimmy Got Gat

18 Metres   5.10b   ★ ★

Climb the white corner at the left
end of the face. This route has fun
moves and good stemming.
Follows six bolts; lower off the
super shuts at the top. FA: R. Reed,
T. Free, Oct ober, 1998; FFA: R.
Reed, S. Charlton.

15 Ghetto Bird

18 Metres   5.8   ★

This route runs straight up the
arête between "Jimmy Got Gat" and
the bolted black face of "Prison
Sex." Pass a fixed piton on the
upper end of the arête before finishing at the super shuts on "Jimmy
Got Gat." FFA: (onsight) J. Hammerich, M. Pellett, October 2000.

16 Prison Sex   20 Metres   5.12a   ★ ★

This crimpy, wicked route with six bolts is about 2 degrees past vertical, and can be
wet in spring. The steep black face has a
number of horizontal cracks and fissures,
topped with a very small roof, on the far left
side of "Fire In Me Eye." Lower off of super
shuts. FA: T. Free, Dallas Markall, September,
1999: FFA:Tom Portfors, July 2003.

17 Fire In Me Eye

20 Metres   5.10c   ★ ★

Spot the cave-like hole at the base of this
route, which makes the start very intimidating. Climb from the top of the boulder at the
base to the first bolt and then up through

Jody Bernst has Fire in Me Eye, 5.10c.

Randy Reed leading the FA of
Gang Wars, 5.8.

Rene Lebel

finger ledges on grey rock into
less steep black rock. The route
is equipped with six bolts and
super shuts, and can be wet in
spring. FA: S. Charlton, M.
Pellett, R. Lebel, T. Kenopic;
FFA: S. Charlton.

18 Bad Crack Habit

30 Metres   5.9

This route is in the big chunky
corner crack, and can be soaking
wet in the spring. Take gear to
four inches, and rappel from the
tree. FA: S. Charlton, R. Lebel,
M. Pellett, T. Kenopic, September
1998.

19 Just Another
Drive-by

24 Metres   5.11c   ★ ★ ★

This excellent sustained climb
works up ten bolts on the overhanging face. Climb a series of sloping holds set at
every angle to a rest at a small corner, which continues to the super shuts. FA: R. Reed,
J. Bernst, J. Simms, October, 1998; FFA: J. Bernst, 1999.

20 Gang Wars   26 Metres   5.8    ★ ★

This climb is at the right end of the large west-facing wall, left of "Captain Chronic," in
the crack to the right of the overhanging face. Climb the crack with little difficulty to
the flaring squeeze chimney, which is guarded with several bolts. The route has five
bolts in all. Continuing up the left-arching corner to the belay and a set of top
anchors. FA: R. Reed, R. Lebel, October 1998; FFA: Dylan Cummings, R. Reed.

21 Captain Chronic Tokes Again   15 Metres   5.10c   ★

On the right side of the first wall, left of a birch tree, climb the crack and a series
ledges. The route has are six bolts and rappel hangers. FA: M. Pellett, S. Charlton,
Trevor Kenopic, R. Lebel, September 1998; FFA: M. Pellett, S. Charlton.

Steve Charlton on Getting Schooled, 5.11+.

The Doughnut Wall

22 My Blueberry Fritter

15 Metres   5.9

Around from Da Projects to the right of "Captain Chronic Tokes Again." Climb the corner crack to a broken crack system in the face with two bolts, to a small roof and then onto the ledge. FA: Brandon Pullan; FFA: Brandon Pullan, Derek Patola, August 2004.

The Schoolhouse

23 Getting Schooled
(2 Pitches)   60 Metres   5.11+

 ★ ★ ★

This route is around the corner on the left edge of The Schoolhouse. In addi-

tion to a standard trad rack, extra small TCU's are useful.

Pitch 1: (5.11c, 40 metres) Climb the stunning crack splitting the largest section of the buttress. Exit the crack, traversing left under the roof, to climb up and left to the belay on the ledge under a square roof.

Pitch 2: (5.11b, 20 metres) From the belay, break into the upper section of the flaring crack. Exit right to the belay. FA: R. Reed, S. Charlton. 2001; FFA: (pitch 1) R.Reed, (pitch 2) S. Charlton, 2003.

Jody Bernst at the high point of the incomplete Graduation Day.

Dylan Cummings just past the crux on Pitch 1 of Expulsion, 5.10c.

24 Graduation Day

18 Metres   5.10+

This is an open project. Straight up the four bolts to the roof, you can see a fixed stopper and a draw suggesting a possible completion to pitch one through a laybacking roof. At present, this route stops at the bolt before the roof, but work is continuing. FA: S. Charlton, R. Reed.

25 Expulsion (2 Pitches)

40 Metres 5.10c

Though the first pitch goes, Pitch Two is still an open project.

Pitch 1: Work up the left-facing corner/flake system for 12 metres to some tense moves just below the roof and some bomber hand jugs. Delicately traverse right around a corner, past a pin, to a committing right hand reach. Passing two more bolts takes you to the belay.

Pitch 2: Continue up through the roof past the quick draw. The second pitch is incomplete. Rappel off of highest bolt. FA: (pitch 1) J. Bernst, D. Cummings.

Big Rig Wall

This is the slab just left of The Schoolhouse.

26 Plains, Trains and Automobiles (4 Pitches?)   75 Metres 5.7

This long face/slab line is a work in progress. When completed, it should be a fun, easy lead using gear to four inches, slings on the trees, a couple of pins; all that fun alpine stuff. FA: B. Pullan (solo).

*Jeff Hammerich on the FA of
Thursday Night Whore, 5.8.*

Mount Olympus

These first three routes can be found by
hiking to the end of the main trail, bushwhacking up to the wall, then working
back south along the base of the cliff until
just before the rock deteriorates to rubble.
The routes are here at the south end.

27 The Mistress

25 Metres   5.10c   ★

Follow the dihedral straight up, just to the
left of "Thursday Night Whore" and finish
at same belay. FA: T. Oliver, J. Hammerich,
M. Pellett, 2001.

28 Thursday Night Whore
(see cover photo)

25 Metres   5.8    ★★★

This is the best 5.8 route in Orient Bay. It is located just left of the amphitheatre.
Climb in the corner up to the slab and crack, trending slightly to the left on the left
face of the corner. There is a rappel station at the top. FA: J. Hammerich, T. Oliver,
M. Pellett, September, 2000.

29 The Third Head of Cerberus 40 Metres   5.10   ★

This route is on the north side of the buttress. It ascends a white corner visible from
the road at about two-thirds height. Take gear to five inches; there is a rappel station at
the top of the first pitch. The second pitch has seen some cleaning and has two bolts at
the top, but is mediocre climbing. FA: R. Reed, M. Pellett, September 2000;
FFA: R. Reed, S. Charlton.

30 The Landmark 90 Metres   5.?   ★★★

This is the most distinct crack through the roof on this wall. It isn't clear who first
climbed the first pitch route to the roof. The pitches above are unclimbed as of yet,
and they look outstanding, although they'll take lots of cleaning. FA: S. Parent? Or
Kevin Crow and Glen ?

31 Passage to Valhalla (3 pitches)   90 Metres   5.12?   ★★★

Work is still continuing on this closed project, but it has every sign of being a stellar
route.

Randy Reed on Passage to Valhalla.

RANDY REED

Pitch 1: (5.12, Trad) From the corner capped by a small roof, bust out laybacking up a steep tips-only crack to a slanting, deep, flaring crack that narrows as it reaches the belay.

Pitch 2: (5.10) Work up the face with a crack, which has one bolt (so far).

Pitch 3: (5.12?) Climb the scoop and corner system, in mixed style. FA: (Pitch 1) T. Free, (Pitch 2) R. Reed , (Pitch 3) S. Charlton, September, 1999.

32 Clash of the Titans (2 Pitches)
70 Metres   5.11a

 ★★★

This route is in the big orange dihedral visible from the road, near the right side of the cliff.

Pitch 1: (5.11, 40 metres) The first pitch is trad style with three pins on the crux before the belay.

Pitch 2: (5.8, 30 metres) Work up easier ground to the top. FA: J. Bernst, R.Reed, August 2000; FFA: J. Bernst, R. Reed.

33 Off-width Crack   ?m   5.?

 ★

This route (and the next) start on the ledge above and to the right of "Clash of the Titans." FA: Alex Boileau, Lee ?

34 Sport Climb   ?m   5.?

Start on the ledge up and right from "Clash of the Titans." FA: Alex Boileau, Lee ?

35 New Route   45 Metres   5.10 or 5.8, A1   ★

Follows a hand crack. FA: M. Pellett, N. Buda, October 2000; FFA: S. Charlton, J. Bernst.

Reflection Wall as seen from Highway 11.

Reflection Wall

In the summer, this solid black wall looks like a fantastic place for several great sport climbs. However, in the winter Reflection Wall is draped with the heinous ice route of the same name (WI5). The local consensus is that to bolt this wall would ruin the nature of the ice climb (first climbed 20 years ago), not to mention the havoc it would wreak on bolts! Thus the wall has and should be left untouched.

Reflection Wall is impossible to miss, less than 2 km north of the trailhead to Taj Mah Wall, as you drive north on Highway 11. That is, it is approximately 5 km north of the compressor station. A trail leads directly from the road down into the gully and up to the wall. While the wall is less then a kilometre from the road, the going can get a little steep. These routes ascend the chimney around the right side of the main wall. Eric and Mickey Landmann, Steve Frye, and John Mattes explored the area in 1999. Landmann and Frye made a trail to the base, working through the boulderfield and hacking through the poison ivy grove. They then cleaned and put up these two ventures.

36 Search and Rescue   27 Metres   5.7   ★

A reasonably fun, easy chimney with good gear. Named for the mission that Eric was on, to save the climbers atop "Don't Go There!." There are some loose chockstones and holds. The upper six feet of the route is extremely rotten rock, but there is gear available. Take care when topping out (at a rap station) or you will bean your belayer. It's hard to handle the rubble, since it is very brushy on top FA: Eric Landmann, August, 1999.

ERIC LANDMANN

*Eri Landmann on the FA of
Search and Rescue, 5.7.*

37 Don't Go There!

25 Metres   5.7

Ten metres right of the chimney,
this manky little mixed climb
abounds with loose gravel, bad
plants and a huge top block that
may not even be there any
longer. Bold, ambitious, ignorant
and foolhardy. It's just a dirty little secret that need not be repeat-
ed. FA: Steve Frye, John Mattes,
August, 1999.

The Tongue/
Spy Wall

The tongue is left (north) of
Reflection Wall where a pointed
slab that resembles a tongue runs two-thirds of the way up the cliffline. "Double
Agent" works straight up the middle of the tongue. These two routes have poison ivy
at the base, and are best climbed in the fall, after a frost.

38 Double Agent   35 Metres   5.8   ★

Go straight up the tongue, to a bolt belay. FFA; (onsight) J. Hammerich, Andrew
Abbink.

39 On the Run With Bin Laden (2 Pitches)   5.9   ★ ★

The first ascendants found 30 feet of poison ivy blocking the approach from any angle;
now that's an objective hazard! It is best to do this climb in the fall, after 9/11. It's
worth it; this line has two pitches of superb climbing.

Pitch 1: (5.9) This amazing Squamish-like slab climbing has two bolts and other gear
placements where you need them. The belay (ring bolts) is on a huge ledge.

Pitch 2: (5.9) An exceptionally gymnastic trad pitch, with a bolt to protect the exit
(crux) moves. FA: J. Hammerich, M. Pellet, 1999?

Mahkwa Buttress

The Mahkwa Buttress is directly across the road from the Reflection Lake Cabins. And that's directly across; the cliff is only 20 feet off the highway. Don't jam up the driveway at the resort. There is a parking area about 100 metres south, near Cascade Falls. This buttress has not been climbed extensively, and still has a lot of loose rock. Routes are described left to right. The first three three climbs are on the north-facing exposure of the cliff above a talus slope.

40 Split Tips   20 Metres   5.10a

A fun crack line. There are ring anchors established for rappel, that will also serve for a toprope anchor. FA: D. Benton, J. Hammerich, 2001.

41 Antifreeze   15 Metres   5.10c

Pitch 1: This is a trad chimney, with rappel station.

Pitch 2: Climb the 5.10 offwidth and traverse the small ledge. Mantle a larger ledge to finish at the top of "Split Tips." A #5 Camalot is very nice.

FA (Pitch 1): D. Benton, J. Hammerich, W. Meinen, J. Bamfield, 2001

FA (Pitch 2): W. Meinen, J. Bryant, Fall 2005.

42 Obsidian Oblivion   20 Metres   5.11a   ★

This stellar crack demands some razor-sharp moves. There are ring anchors on top of the pillar. FA: D. Benton, J. Hammerich, 2001.

43 Bonsai   20 Metres   5.7

This little line is a blocky wander up to a slung cedar tree. FA: J. Bamfield, W. Meinen, 2001.

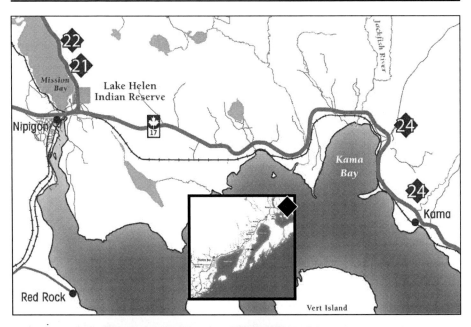

24 Kama Bay

Route Character Sport – 1, Trad – 2, Multi-pitch – 1

Difficulty		
	5.8–	0
	5.9	1
	5.10	1
	5.11+	1

Getting There: From Nipigon, drive east, and continue east on Highway 17 when Highway 11 splits off to go to Orient Bay. About 20 kilometres from Nipigon (about one and a half hours out of Thunder Bay), the massive western exposure of the Kama Hills will loom in the windshield. Turn left onto Domtar 81 road, and go just under 2 km (past the "Crown Land" sign) to a brown post. This marks the trail to the "Getting Oriented" ice area, which is about half an hour in from the road.

The western exposure of the Kama Hills holds more than 20 ice routes, up to 70 metres tall, on its wild, high walls. The one exploratory summer trip (so far) tagged three substantial rock climbs. Do the math.

Many ice climbers know of the spectacular routes to be found in Kama Bay. However, in the warmer months it has just as much to offer, if not more. Andre Van Schaik, Joanne Parent-Murphy and Shaun Parent did two routes above the gravel pit on Highway 17 (about a half-mile past the Kama Bay lookout) sometime in the 80's.

Will Mienen and Andy Gallant went back in the spring of 2004, and then Brandon Pullan and Noel Gingrich went later in the summer, to see what could be found on the walls themselves. They started in on three big towers that look like they are from some mythical story about dragons and orcs. They can be seen from the highway.

The Towers

1 Pineapple Express (3 pitches) 90 Metres 5.9 R/X ★ ★

Pitch 1: Start on the right side of the central tower into the obvious weakness, which ends at a spacious ledge, clipping two fixed pins along the way. Have gear to make a belay.

Pitch 2: Climb straight up for a short second pitch to a two-bolt anchor on another ledge.

Pitch 3: Traverse around an airy, exposed corner to an exceptional finger crack, which leads to the top.

The first ascent took gear from RP's to a #3 Camalot. Rappel off the slung boulder at the top to the bolts, and from there to the ground. FA; (ground-up, on-sight) W. Meinen and A. Gallant, Spring 2004.

2 Cracktastic (2 pitches)   45 Metres   5.10b ★ ★

Start in the spicy dihedral, work through a small roof, and then plunge into an absolutely amazing finger-to-hand-to-fist crack. Then wander up the slab (as a second pitch) to the top. Takes gear to three inches. FFA: (ground-up, on-sight) W. Meinen, A. Gallant, Spring 2004.

3 Whiskey on the Rocks   30 Metres   5.11a ★ ★

This route is near the pillars, but tough to find. Just right of the third pillar, this line of 13 bolts follows easy holds to steep finish. Rappel from bolts on the ledge. FFA: B. Pullan, N. Gingrich, Summer 2004.

25 Neys Provincial Park

Route Character Sport – 0, Trad – 1, Mixed – 0, Toprope – 0,Multi-pitch – 1

Difficulty	
5.8–	1
5.9	0
5.10	0
5.11+	0

Getting There: Take Highway 11/17 east from Thunder Bay past Terrace Bay until you come upon Neys Provincial Park (22 km west of Marathon, and about two and a half hours from Thunder Bay) on the south (lake) side of the highway. The route is located on the cliffs on the west side of the Pic River (just west of the camping area). Park at the west end of the bridge over the Little Pic River and follow an old road north along the cliff base

This area, for all is ease of access, seems remote, being just outside of a provincial park in a stretch off the Trans Canada highway that is sparsely populated.

Access Issues

This climb is located just outside Neys Provincial Park on Crown land.

Camping

Neys Provincial Park – on the beach adjacent to the route.

Swimming

The park has a fantastic shallow sandy beach for swimming, although Lake Superior is cold at any time of year.

1 **Prisoner of War** (3 pitches)   100 Metres   5.8

This route is the summer complement of the ice climb "Ice Pic." Both lie on the huge rock face on the northwest side of the Little Pic River just west of the provincial park. The climb starts with clean rock and a crux right at the start of the first pitch. It then becomes progressively easier and dirtier for the second and third pitches. This route is (presumably) named for Neys' role as a POW camp for German WWII prisoners.
FA: Albert Chong, D. Nix, F. Pianka, 1994.

NICK BUDA

NICK BUDA

NICK BUDA

194

Rappelling off Totem Pole Wall.

BRANDON PULLAN

7 Squaw Bay — *Scott Kress cleaning P2 of American Demon.*

SHAUN PARENT

9 The Bluffs — *Shawn Robinson on the nose of Zig Zag.*

NICK BUDA

197

9 The Bluffs   *Shawn Robinson on the start of Oltenrec.*

NICK BUDA

NICK BUDA

Derrik Patola under the Block of Death.

NICK BUDA

NICK BUDA

12 Silver Harbour *Steven Gale on Greco.*

12 Silver Harbour *Shawn Robinson on Huber Goes to Yosemite.*

NICK BUDA

NICK BUDA

Mark Powell near the top of Cliffhanger.

NICK BUDA

15 Pass Lake

Mike Holowaty on Cave Crawler.

15 Pass Lake

Mike Holowaty on the face of Flying Circus.

20 Claghorn *Shawn Robinson takes up the Ace of Swords.*

21 Orient Bay *Patrick Martel alongside the Great Pinnacle.*

Thunder Bay Rock

Index